THERE IS A PLACE
WHERE YOU
ARE NOT ALONE

THERE IS A PLACE WHERE YOU ARE NOT ALONE

Hugh Prather

A DOLPHIN BOOK
Doubleday & Company, Inc.
Garden City, New York
1980

DESIGNED BY MARILYN SCHULMAN

ISBN 0-385-14778-3
Library of Congress Catalog Card Number: 80-912

Copyright © 1980 by Hugh Prather

Printed in the United States of America
First Edition

To my sons

AN ACKNOWLEDGMENT

If it is possible to know such things, I know that Gayle Prather, my wife, is my spiritual partner. Everything I have written in the last twelve years has been half hers because we have taken each step together, even when we thought we were far apart. Thank you, Gayle. And I thank God for His endless gift.

TO THE READER

Because there is a place in me, I know there is a place in you where you are not alone. This book is about how I once again came to that place, but this time I did not turn away. It is not a detailed account of how I arrived there, but merely a tracing of some of the actual footsteps that led me there. It contains a few key events and many of the thoughts that followed. As usual, I have left the transitions out and the inconsistencies in. I hope my description reminds you of a journey very much like your own, because now I know we walk together. Only the words we use to describe it will differ, but words will not change our direction or our deep need of each other along the way.

I have worried about how you will react to this. I have imagined that you would have one of two perceptions of this book. The first is that most of what I have written is so self-deceived as to be fundamentally out of touch with reality. I might have viewed it as such probably as little as five years ago. The change in me is not so much an increase in wisdom as it is a new willingness to look at what else I believe, and to use those terms that seem to me most appropriate. So to you who may react in this first way, I want you to know that this book does not contain everything I believe, and certainly little of how I act, but it does hint at the direction I am now attempting to walk, however haltingly. This book is what I think can be seen by anyone, and what I believe I have in fact seen.

The second perception I imagine your having is one that recognizes the enormous distance I have yet to go. I am not so fearful of this because I know that an accurate perception is also truly helpful. One of the side roads along our way is a certain competitiveness in mystical or spiritual experiences, a reverence for the form to the exclusion of content. My public role in life seems to be that of an ordinary person who can write about his ordinariness. In talking to others, I find that my spiritual experiences are also quite familiar to anyone who has seen his direction and begun to pray or meditate deeply in his own behalf. I have had only one experience that might be called a "vision." And although I have at times felt communicated with, I have not yet heard a voice that did not on one level seem like my own thought. But there have been some personal surprises, and I will talk about some of those shortly.

What I present here is given primarily with the desire to be supportive of those of you who are at a similar spot on the road to mine, and not, I hope, calculated to impress you with my uniqueness, although I cannot promise you that I will not at times be influenced by that desire.

As we are to each other, so is God to us. If I separate myself from you by believing that I have some special spiritual connection, I have, in my own mind, cut myself off from what joins me to you and therefore to Love itself. If light allows us to see the spiritual, it must also provide the gentle recognition of what encircles us both. It must shine on the road we walk and show us how blessed we are to travel together.

Hugh Prather
May 31, 1980
Santa Fe, New Mexico

AUTHOR'S NOTE

This book is organized as follows: The first section gives a few of the mystical or spiritual experiences that accompanied certain changes in my thinking. The second section contains many of those new thoughts. The third section shows examples of how they can be applied. And the fourth section provides a few practice exercises or prayers. The brief discussions of crisis situations, such as suicide, child abuse and the others found in the third section, come from the work I have been doing over the past ten years. These are not intended to answer all the questions raised in these fields. The ideas are only the ones I myself have found helpful and do not include many concepts effectively used by others. They are given here as possible starting points to the reader's own thinking.

Somewhere in consciousness there lies a land undiscovered, a land not yet revealed by religion, philosophy, or science. I know that it exists for it continually pushes itself into my awareness. I know that when it discloses itself, it will change the nature of mankind: wars will be no more, and the lamb will lie down with the lion.

Joel Goldsmith
A Parenthesis in Eternity

This world is but the dream that you can be alone, and think without affecting those apart from you.

A Course in Miracles

There is a place in you where this whole world has been forgotten; where no memory of sin and of illusion linger still. There is a place in you which time has left, and echoes of eternity are heard.

A Course in Miracles

Experiences

After I had written Notes on Love and Courage I felt that, in some sense, my life was now finished. It seemed to me that within the three diaries I had published over the last ten years, I had said all that I could without merely repeating myself. I felt that my work here was probably done and, very often during those first few months, I found myself waiting to die.

It was not a morbid period. I have had a few suicidal times in my life and know what those are like. It was more a feeling that ran like this: "I think I have done the best I could, considering my limitations. So if there is anyone up there in charge of my departure, I want you to know I feel finished and relatively comfortable about leaving." But nothing happened.

Then one day I got violently sick. It occurred quite suddenly. I hardly had enough strength to get to my bed, but after a few hours I felt strong enough to attempt taking a hot bath, which I thought might ease the pain I was in. My tub is over six feet long and very deep. I filled it, and after soaking for maybe half an hour I tried climbing back up the two steps that lead to it. The last thing I remembered was standing on the top step, reaching for a towel. When I came to, perhaps twenty or thirty minutes later, Gayle was calling to me. I blacked out again before she was finally able to get me out of the water. Although I was still sick and was now bleeding from a blow to my head, the one thought that dominated all others was the seeming impossibility that I had not sunk underwater and drowned.

If there really was a time to go, apparently mine had not yet come. But what else in life was there for me to do except make the same tired attempts to learn the same old lessons? I didn't have too long to wait for an answer.

Now, as I look back at that time, I realize that, instead of having learned all I could, I had not even begun. I had only reached a certain willingness to begin. I now wanted to take the first step on the "journey of a thousand miles." As I write this, about three years from that time, I feel as though I have taken perhaps two or three steps, and the distance yet to travel seems impossibly long. I find that I frequently give up and try to retreat. Yet there is a sanity in me which reminds me that to regret that a journey wasn't started earlier only delays further its beginning.

What I did next was a mistake. And I see now

it had to be done in order for me to know why it was a mistake. I took things into my own hands. In effect I said, "Now I see what the plan is, and I'll take over from here." I was to do this on a large scale one more time [I will get to that a little later] before I began to see even a glimmering of what it means to trust the course of your life. Trust is just another way of defining the thousand-mile journey.

I assumed that I was going to be around for possibly another twenty or thirty years [for what reason I did not know, but by now I had a definite feeling that something more was yet to come, a feeling I could not account for by just a fall in a tub]. I reasoned that I had better start preparing myself, and so I began a program to get into the best shape physically and mentally I could, and, along with it, to open up areas of talent I had some reason to suspect I had.

I made a list of every way I wanted to improve and of all the new areas I wanted to develop. I allotted so many minutes to each category until I had filled an eight-hour schedule. For example: Sculpting: 1 hour; Writing: 2 hours; Being a Saint [doing something for someone else without his or anyone else's knowledge]: ½ hour; Exercise: 2 hours; Aberrations [doing something totally out of character]: ½ hour; and so forth.

I quickly found that something would usually come up during the day that would keep me from getting through the list. Consequently, I was repeating the first few activities and seldom getting to those at the end. So I decided to redefine the word "day" to let it mean whatever length of time it took me to accomplish what I wanted to. It often required two or three solar days to do this, and then I would start a new "day."

After I had lived that way for a few weeks, certain activities began to "take over." For example, I started spending more and more time sculpting and painting, whereas the time I had set aside to study, say, Latin went consistently unused. Also, I was deeply impressed with the effects on my mental state of the half hour spent "Being a Saint." Just one pure intention, without the expectation of even gratitude in return, would at times make everything in my experience glow gently and warmly for hours. I remember wondering what it would be like to devote one's entire life to this approach, but I made no attempt to try it for even a day.

During this time I began to feel a strong urge to do something on behalf of "Notes on Love and Courage." The only thing I could think of was to go on a promotional tour, and that, I believed, would be a form of prostitution. I had made very few public appearances up to then and had in fact turned down all invitations outside a small radius around Santa Fe.

However, the urge I felt persisted. It was the kind of feeling I had written about in my books and had advised others to follow. It was strong and calm, a gentle but persistent nudging. During this period of conflict over whether or not to go, something happened that was so unexpected that if journeys begin with a single step this was probably my first.

I wish the little story that follows were more elegant. I realize it is a ludicrous way to have the course of one's life changed, but it is simply the way it happened. Why it affected me so deeply may be hard to understand. Part of the explanation is that the words I was given took me straight back to a time when I had felt a deep conviction about the purpose of my life. I was being called on to keep an old promise.

Gayle and I had just met Dan and Dory, and they invited us to dinner. We were joined by a friend of theirs named Dee who had recently come to town. It was the first time they had seen her since the three of them had shared a house together.

They told us that after dinner they planned

to do a "procedure" which used to help them be less afraid when they had lived together. They described it and said they would like Gayle and me to join them if we wanted to. We said yes, and so after dinner we all went into their kitchen and sat around a table.

Dee tore up pieces of paper and wrote out the letters of the alphabet, the words "yes" and "no," and the numbers zero through nine, and put them on the table in a large circle. The five of us then stacked our hands on top of an empty water glass which had been turned upside down in the center of the circle.

Dory, who was the "facilitator," closed her eyes and asked if there were any messages for anyone. The glass immediately began circling within the ring of papers with extraordinary force, and then indicated there was a message for Gayle.

Dory asked what it was, and the glass spelled out the words "Your function is to love."

I asked who the message was from. The answer was "J.C." I said, "Does that stand for Jesus Christ?" The glass went to "yes."

At this point the entire situation took on a certain light absurdity for me. I was fairly certain that Dory was the one moving the glass, even if she wasn't doing it consciously. She had exhibited a suspicious liking for unusual happenings, having already claimed to have seen a UFO on two occasions, and yet she appeared honest and natural, so I assumed she was merely tricking herself.

Then the glass indicated it had a message for me. It was "Do go." This startled me because no one else at the table, except possibly Gayle, should have had any way of knowing what that meant. I didn't think the other three people were even aware that I was a writer, but if that were not so, they certainly would have no way of knowing I had been wrestling with that question.

After I explained to them what the "Do go" meant, Dory asked if there were any further messages for me. "Yes," indicated the glass, and spelled out, "Love man." Dory asked if there was anything more. "Yes. Please love man." She said she was sure I understood the message and was there anything else. "Yes. Do go." And so it went, over and over, the same words: "Love man." "Please go." "Please love man," for what seemed like an hour or hour and a half.

During this time, people would get tired and remove their hands, so that at some moments only I or only Gayle and I had our hands on the glass, and yet it continued to move exactly as before.

Finally, Dory said, "Please tell us how many

previous lives he has had." The glass went to "zero."

Seemingly paying no attention to that answer, she asked, "When did he die last?" The glass spelled out "1957." "Oh," she said, "that's a mistake." "No," I told her. "That was the year I gave up my boyhood religion. And in those days, the way I frequently expressed my religious conviction to myself was to think, 'I only have one thing to do in life and that is to love man.' "

Then the glass went to the number "eight" and spelled out, "Great joy." It did this several times, repeating the number "eight" and the word "joy."

It was not until two years later that I had my first unusual experience with that number. It was in connection with the birth of our son, John, who had so many eights associated with the time between his conception and birth that it became a running joke that repeatedly delighted us.

Since then there have been other experiences with eight, all gentle and happy moments and always unanticipated. I have no idea what that number means. I remember nothing unusual in my life associated with eight, and numerology has been of no interest to me.

As Gayle and I drove back from Dan and Dory's home, we asked each other what had actually happened and what did it all mean. Neither of us really knew. I was left with nothing more concrete than that I had been communicated with by something that knew me very intimately. I felt loved and looked after, but by what I did not know. The one thing I could feel with certainty was that a circle had been completed and that I would never be the same again.

In the weeks that followed I tried to pray in the way I had as a boy, but I felt awkward and dishonest. I also tried praying to whatever had communicated with me that evening. I found myself saying silly things like, "Whoever you are, I hope I'm not disturbing you, but I would like to know what I'm supposed to do now."

I finally gave all that up and started working each morning on a list of qualities or attributes toward which my life seemed to be moving me. For some time I had been feeling a growing conviction that all events had a direction. Life could be thought of as a type of spiritual evolution. For example, I had noticed how I and others, as time passed, were becoming more sensitive to other people's pain and less willing to harm anything at all. This was not a shared philosophical position but an instinctive transformation. It seemed a very slow but unmistakable process.

I felt that whatever had "spoken" to me was already at the point toward which I was only moving. But I did not know what to do about that, and my efforts to contact it only frustrated me. If, however, I was evolving toward it, possibly there was a way I could get behind my own evolution. In an attempt to do that, I began thinking every morning about the qualities I had so far identified. I would ask myself what it meant to be honest, open, gentle, patient, pure and so forth. I would simply let my mind dwell on each one, and I would often write down what occurred to me.

I was already doing this when I went on my first small promotional tour. I had always assumed that I would be unable to write while traveling and appearing on talk shows, etc., but in those two weeks I did more writing than at any other comparable period in my life.

After I would finish with my morning meditation on a now growing list of qualities, I would feel as if I had been lifted an inch or two off the ground, and the entire day would continue like a gentle walk with friends down some lovely beach. Everywhere I went I found I wanted to talk about basic goodness: fairness, humanity, goodwill. It seemed that within a few simple qualities could be found our entire way out.

After the second small tour, I was back in Santa Fe with nothing further scheduled. I had signed a two-book contract with my publisher, and the first book was not due for about two years. So I mentally sat back and waited to see what would happen next.

Very shortly I was introduced to a book entitled "The Spiritual Journey of Joel Goldsmith." Books seek us out. They slip themselves into our hands just at the time we are ready for a new self-concept. For me, this book served the purpose of suggesting a way of meditating or praying that I knew I could try with enthusiasm. I have never liked the techniques or procedures that are usually taught as an essential part of meditation, and I have already noted the problems I had with my boyhood form of prayer. This, however, was the simplest and most direct approach I had read.

It had evidently just occurred to Joel Goldsmith one day to try sitting in a chair and listening. Nothing more than that. He would usually do this for only a few minutes, then get up and go about his work. When he felt like doing it again, he would, but only for as long as made him happy. By the end of the day he would ordinarily have taken ten, twenty, thirty or more of these prayer breaks, but this large number was not a goal he set in advance.

When I started trying something similar myself, often I was not aware of any unusual occurrences during those times or of any special results afterward, but eventually a moment would come when something so not-of-this-world would intrude itself that I would at times find myself questioning my own sanity.

It seemed inappropriate to speak of these experiences to anyone. Even the thought of doing so felt somehow irreverent or sacrilegious. And I was also afraid of what others might think of me. The underlying rapture of the experience itself was unmistakable, but there were moments when I was distressed over what I suspected was happening to my mind, and yet I felt a powerful urgency to continue. I had to sit in that chair. It was as though I were being carried along by a shift in the direction of my planet.

Now that I have met many others who have had these types of experiences, I realize that mine were fairly typical, even commonplace, within the context of meditation or deep prayer. Once again, I seem to be an ordinary person whose work is to write about his ordinariness, and I wish to share these experiences with you because I am convinced that if you haven't already, you will eventually go through something very similar. There is no reason why anyone should feel guilt or painful self-doubt over what is a natural process of growth.

The first surprising thing that happened was that I went through a period of a few weeks during which I felt as though I were being given dictation. It was an internal impression of words rather than a sound. I wrote profusely, especially during or just after my period of quiet listening. I considered the material a combination of thoughts I "heard" interwoven with my own thoughts.

I now believe that my sitting in a chair and listening did not cause what happened. Doing that simply gave form to my decision to hear, and similar experiences can occur, and do occur for others, at any time, under any circumstances, whether one is awake or asleep. Nothing needs to be done in order to experience a radically different perception of reality. It comes the instant it is wanted, and the context in which it occurs does not trigger it.

I have also noticed that the manner in which new perceptions come is personally symbolic to the individual. Some people will be "told" to turn to a book, some will see images, some "hear" a voice, others will simply have a calm sense of direction with no worded concept attached. In looking back, it does not surprise me that my first lessons came through my pencil.

This is the first idea I wrote down, and I wrote it over and over in varying forms for possibly a week: "Do what you want, you can't make a mistake." The statement seemed patently absurd and I argued with it every time it came. I could think of endless examples of mistakes. And surely some further restraint on my behavior was needed than just doing what I wanted. I remember one evening in particular when I was "receiving" this message again and was objecting very strongly to the concept, I suddenly heard, "If you would rather say: Do what you really want. You can't make a mistake." Oh. "Do what you really want" is what I had been advising in every book I had written. Was it possible there was no degree of wanting, no shallow vs. deep desire, that there was only one will and that everyone did in fact do what he wanted to, and what he did was precisely what needed to be done in the context of some larger purpose or overall view of his life?

I will not pursue this line of thought here because I still, three years later, have some difficulty with this concept. It is simply the first thing that came. I will leave it to you to determine if it is helpful.

Other thoughts that have come in this manner I have included in the section that follows. No concept is true. A concept is always a partial perception. A "good" concept simply allows me to see more than before. It will soon be replaced by other words, if words are what is needed, that allow my mind an even greater scope. The word "God," repeated in stillness and comfort, becomes an anthem which encompasses and constitutes all.

I will describe a few other unusual happenings that occurred during meditation or prayer, but I should mention here the second time I made, on a grand scale, the mistake of taking my spiritual program into my own hands, because it happened at about this time.

It started when I looked at the activities of my life in terms of benefits and disadvantages. I began adding up the pluses and minuses of everything I did and then eliminating anything that was not clearly beneficial. I stopped running, playing tennis, watching television, eating meat and sugar, drinking alcohol, going to movies, going to parties, and on and on. What didn't occur to me was that nothing in the world is clearly beneficial. No activity looked at in this manner will add up to even so much as an escape from boredom. So many things I thought I could rely on to please me in some way, when examined thoroughly and honestly, failed to hold up: going out with certain friends, eating certain foods, sleep, exercise, sexual fantasies, physical superiority, professional accomplishments, knowledge, adulation, marriage, friendship, psychic powers, even spiritual or mystical experiences as special events.

This process of housecleaning continued until one day I was reading a book—another example of the book appearing when the reader is ready—entitled "A Course in Miracles" (actually, a set of three books), and I realized that it is literally impossible to know in advance what is in your best interest. I slammed down the book and ran to the garden, where Gayle was watering, and shouted, "It is impossible to decide beforehand what is best. It simply can't be done. Vegetarianism is a decision. Let's go to the Steaksmith." Which we did.

Since then, I have resumed doing some of the things I had given up and others have remained discarded. But none of that, in itself, has any importance. I now believe that neither indulgence nor abstinence has real value. What indicates value is the honest answer to the question, "What is this for?" Tennis, for example, is not a selfish activity, nor is it unselfish. The question "Why am I on this tennis court?" points to what is motivating me, and, seeing that, I can choose to follow the leadings of harmlessness and peace and so make of this moment a gift.

By this time I was using the word "God" in my meditations. It was the only word large enough to fit the presence of what I would sometimes feel. By "God" I know I mean at least this much: It is that which is wholly harmless and fair, a presence available to all, and in all, which never guides through punishment or force, and which is so vast and so entirely kind that all attempts at description seem merely silly.

My next experience came one night after I had called a friend. He lived in another part of the country and we had not seen each other for over ten years, but I had thought of him during all of this because of the type of discussions we used to have. I believed I had now come around to some of his views and that we would have much to talk about.

The desire to talk to others about deep personal experiences of this sort often contains an apparently innocent denial of the very truth that has been seen. I can't remember a single time that it has given me or others I know who have tried it the satisfaction that it appeared to offer. It is similar to an alcoholic celebrating his New Year's resolution to give up drinking by getting drunk. It is not dangerous. The truth seen will not go away. But it is often only our ego's attempt to capitalize on the very incident that allowed us to see the ego's lack of value. If, for example, a moment comes in which I glimpse the unity of all life, and then I run to a friend and say, in effect, "You'll never guess what happened to me!" my behavior denies that I believe he and I have always been together and all I have of value, he has with me. And if I double the mistake by trying to convince him of the truth of what I have seen, I will appear, for the moment, to lose the beauty I saw.

Natural moments of sharing will occur in their own time. But the excited recounting of a spiritual experience will accomplish what it is intended to. And if the purpose is to give the appearance of having been singled out and set apart, then the resulting feeling will be one of loneliness and separation, not communication and joining.

My conversation with my old friend was horrible. Every idea I presented him he rejected, and he urged me to read certain writings which would correct my muddy thinking. I finally began agreeing with him in a dishonest attempt to gain the appearance of mutual understanding. Afterward I was so shaken that I began to doubt the very things I had experienced. I had recognized the possibility that every concept I had was wrong.

All day, following the conversation, my feeling of confusion and distress grew. That night as I sat in my chair, I began pleading with God to tell me something, anything, just one simple truth. Now there were books to write and speeches to give, and yet I knew nothing. If I had no idea of what was going on out there, how could I in honesty stand before an audience and make statements? "Give me just one truth," I begged. And so it went for the entire night. First I would listen, then cry and plead. But nothing seemed to be happening despite my loud desperation.

At daybreak, I finally said to God, "I am not going to leave this chair until you tell me something. This is not fair. What am I going to tell these people who have asked me to speak to them? If I must, I will sit here until I die. What possible purpose would there be in my continuing?" Still, no answer appeared to come.

Suddenly I became very tired. I knew I couldn't remain in the chair. I said to God, "I am going over and lie on the couch, but I am not going to leave this room. You must tell me something." I had visions of Gayle pushing food under the door and my refusing to eat it.

But as I lay there I became intensely hungry. What was God doing? I was being left with no pride at all, and a very serious situation was becoming funny. I mustered all the seriousness I could and said, "I am going into the kitchen to get something to eat, but I will never leave this house. I will stay here until I die unless you tell me something."

Two days before, Gayle and I had picked up a stray dog on the highway. She had not left my side day or night since then. She wouldn't go outside or continue eating unless I stayed with her. And yet, all the while, she appeared to be deeply grieving over her abandonment. Every hour or so she would begin moaning and whining like some lost child.

All during this night, she had remained by my feet, but either she had been silent or I had not noticed her crying. While I was in the kitchen, she indicated that she needed to go outside, and it was then that I first realized that something had indeed happened. When I saw her need, I felt within me, for the first time in memory, the quality of harmlessness. I knew, for that instant, I was incapable of hurting her, and I immediately took her outside.

Before, I had thought of harmlessness as merely an absence of certain negative qualities, but this was a feeling of capacity, the capacity to do no harm. I did not retain contact with that feeling for more than a few hours, but that was enough for me to sense the power of true gentleness. I now know that nothing hurtful can stand before it.

When I came back into the house I recognized something else that had been occurring during the night. What I had been asking for was "one simple truth." That sounded innocent, the least I could expect, but now I realized my prayer had not included the audiences I had said I needed something to say to, or the people who would read the books I had agreed to write. It was not: "Please give everyone on this earth one simple truth." If that had been what I had requested, and if it had been given, who would then need someone with private knowledge to stand before him? There would be no audiences and no need for further books if each person on this earth recognized that God Himself was available as his Teacher. That day will come.

All the while I had been listening for a Voice, something far more valuable was being given me, and throughout the night I had chosen to ignore it. Now it all came back.

The pain of doubting everything I had ever thought to be true had been immense. Possibly it was the most shattering experience of my life. I had seen there was no personal basis for knowledge and there never could be. By himself, no one could be certain of anything, and yet who, in his daily life, looked straight at that fact? Certainly I had not. Yet during this "crisis of faith" I had never doubted one thing: There was Something that did know. This I had called God and pleaded that He make an exception in my case and in my terms. The entire experience had been the reverse of a suicidal depression or of the feeling of interminable bleak despair I had experienced at other times in my life. During those times I had still thought I knew something: that reality is uncaring.

All through the night there had been moments when I felt bodily transported to a place where I could see this same struggle again and again. I saw Abraham, having bound his son for sacrifice in order to extract an answer from God, on his knees, crying, begging God to tell him something, anything. I saw Moses in the desert, waving his hands toward heaven, pleading with God to tell him something, anything, so these people would not think him a lunatic. I saw Mary Baker Eddy pacing up and down her second-floor room, pleading with God, the newspapers of her time screaming that she was mad, and she suspecting they could very well be right. And then I began to see people I had known, and knew now, going through this same crisis. Everyone would have to honestly and bluntly face the truth that he had no way of knowing anything. And this for some would appear to be a devastating ordeal. But it would only be the dawning on his mind of an obvious fact: What we know we know because we are one. In our oneness is perfect knowledge and peace, but in conflict, controversy and specialness there can be only despair. Even though they may choose to hear it at different times, God speaks to all His children at once.

From the time something spoke to me through a moving water glass until the end of the times I would sit in a chair and listen was approximately one year. It was marked by other spiritual fireworks: a few healings, further "dictations," one or two precognitive episodes. It was a time of wonder, and it appeared that the wonder would never stop. But in the two years since then, the nature of the work to be done has changed.

I have already mentioned one type of mistake I made during that first year: trying to assume the role of my own guide or teacher, instead of continuing to consult, moment by moment, decision by decision, the quiet sense of guidance that had brought me this far. A mistake I have not mentioned, one that came later in this period, was my assumption that I had advanced spiritually beyond my friends. My evidence for this was that I couldn't talk to them about these new perceptions. The few attempts I made met with blank stares or nervous chatter. My efforts were accomplishing nothing more than to make us all feel uncomfortable and different from each other. And yet, having the old discussions we had always had was now very tedious for me. Most of our conversations seemed no more than an attempt to come to general agreement on what we all deplored.

There can be no true agreement on what is right and wrong with the world, as any discussion in depth will quickly show. But since everyone knows this, we keep our attacks on food, movies, politicians and football coaches very superficial in order that a fake sense of sharing can be maintained.

Without judgments there would be nothing to talk about, or so it seemed as I would sit there, one moment feeling uncomfortably silent, the next, dishonestly joining in the attack on some mutual acquaintance. There appeared no way out except to make new friends and avoid the old. So I began mentally waiting for these people to pass out of my life. But very few passed.

What I had not yet seen was that my underlying assumption of what was going on was wrong. There were no differences between me and my old friends. Another person is never a hindrance to spiritual growth. If that were possible, it would refute the essence of every spiritual teaching that has come to earth. Another's mind cannot touch mine without mine touching his. If one of us is terrified, we are scared together, even though we may, and probably will, attribute different causes to our fears and express them in radically different ways. The perception of inequality is simple rejection of responsibility. If I claim not to share in the mental state of those around me, I have lost my only way out. "Physician, heal thyself" is the open door to immediate freedom. Forgive and be comfortable and everyone around me sighs with relief, because fear will not continue in the presence of genuine peace.

In these last two years the form of my spiritual journey has changed considerably. I have not completed this stage, and so I will not attempt to describe it fully. It is clear to me that I have increasingly been placed in the role of servant, a supporter of other people's endeavors, and it is also clear that in what has otherwise been a bleak and confusing time, I have felt a growing awareness of the presence of One Who loves me. It is many long moments before dawn, but a soft light is even now spreading over the earth.

I can remember almost the day that what I now think of as the second stage began. It felt as if this Friend who had been so much with me had simply walked out. I had been returned to the first grade with a note that read, "He must do it all again but this time without a tutor." Quite the opposite was happening. I was being shown the vast areas where I was not applying the truths I had been given. Here were the places I was deserting my Friend, not He deserting me. Now the time had come to begin expanding my little area of sanity. The one tool I had was the recognition that I could accomplish nothing by myself and that I must consult directly the

Guide who had brought me this far about every further step to be taken.

I will come back to this point in a few examples given in the second to last section of this book, but here I would like to detail for you how this process of consultation developed for me.

In order to be certain of the accuracy of his decision, one would have to see the circumstances involved without distortion; he would have to foresee all the consequences of his actions; and he would have to know everyone his decision would touch and how it would affect them all. No one would claim such knowledge, and it is therefore understandable why we so often feel anxious while making decisions and guilt over the results. Only a moment's honest reflection is needed to recognize that there is simply no way of knowing what course of action would truly be in one's best interests. And yet who has not at some moment in his life felt a gentle urging to take some action that he did not think was reasonable but later events showed was exactly what was needed at the time? What I now see, and what anyone can discover for himself, is that this intuition, this quiet sense of direction, is always present and can be consulted directly. All that is required is the decision to make no further decisions. Once this is done, that which knows the answer will direct every aspect of one's life, appearing to become more clear in its instructions as fear of its misuse lessens. The clarity with which the guidance is heard increases in proportion as fear retreats, because the purpose of the guidance is the release from fear.

I realized that I could not determine by myself what decisions were important or unimportant, spiritual or mundane, for the same reasons that I could not make the decision itself with accuracy and fairness. Therefore, every time I recognized that I was engaged in a decision-making process of any sort, I would ask what to do.

At first, the answer appeared to be quite clear in a few instances, yet absent altogether in most others. To undercut this confusion, whenever I was unsure of the answer, I would ask myself, "What do I honestly believe I have been told to do?" I did not ask "What should I do?" because that calls upon my personal history and not the voice of guidance.

Having asked that question, I would notice a slight leaning or preference, and I would follow it. One may be immobilized by his fear, but his mind is never neutral as to what to do.

If I found I was afraid, I would wait and ask again.

The answer would come to me in different ways. It comes to everyone in a thousand ways if he wishes to look about him, but one way will do. For me, there is usually a sense of an inner tone or light that rises or brightens for "yes" and falls or lessens for "no." The answer that I am to wait is a peaceful absence of both. At other times, the answer has come in different forms: a thought clearly not my own; an urging to open a particular book; an impression of something to be done, for example, to phone someone; a certain lightheartedness that nothing needs to be done; an indication to wait, and then later, while talking to someone, the answer clearly spoken by him, at times so surprisingly direct it appears to be a break in the flow of conversation. On many occasions the answer has come much later in some unexpected and unforeseen form but always recognizable as the answer. Even Jesus did not always get the answer he thought he wanted, nor did it always come at the time he believed he needed it. Note how often he waited.

One insight that greatly strengthened this form of communication was the recognition that I wanted to learn to hear the voice of my inner Teacher more than I wanted to avoid certain impractical or embarrassing results. Whenever I asked myself what I thought was the worst possible consequence of doing what I believed I had been told, I immediately saw how puny was this imagined inconvenience compared to learning to hear the gentle urgings of Love.

What can be said about the characteristics of the answers that I and the many others I know who do this receive? There are at least two that are consistently present. The instruction given calls for no real sacrifice or loss. What may at first appear as certain deprivation is later seen as only the discarding of something that had no worth, with a strong gain of freedom in return. But usually there is not even a momentary perception of loss because the goal is peace, not the increase of fear. Another characteristic is the total absence of harm to others. Especially when it has appeared that whatever action was taken would hurt someone, the Answer would show me a way in which no harm resulted.

To start on this course of actively practicing trust is to exchange a multiplicity of conflicting goals for a single purpose. Now one's objective in everything he does is to hear and follow the leadings of peace. No longer is he afraid he will be asked to lay down his happiness in any activity. That to which he now turns knows what will make him happy and safe in the very way he can understand and appreciate it most. He no longer withholds a single detail of his life from Love, knowing that Love is not requesting of him even a temporary sense of injury. What need is there for Love's gift to be disguised as a punishment and how could this be a fair and reasonable way to teach trust in the only thing that can be trusted?

Of all these happenings, there is one, as yet unmentioned, that is the most important. I cannot tell you exactly when it occurred, but it was well after the fireworks stopped. Possibly it was halfway into the three-year period.

Gayle had supported me in all of this, although at times she seemed shocked at some of the positions I would take regarding our finances, health habits and other matters. But I think a time came when she realized that I was at least acting quite committed and she began to challenge me as to how I knew these seemingly radical concepts were true.

I had long since been through my night of crisis and therefore had already seen that I had no personal way of being certain of anything. And yet I was continuing to act on a set of new assumptions: that one could trust the events of his life; that each person would be provided whatever he needed to do the work he had been given; that the nature of that work was not known or knowable to his ego; that everything he did, every act, thought, fantasy, dream and feeling contributed helpfully and precisely to the overall purpose of his life; that ultimately there were no mistakes in any of this and therefore no grounds for judging himself or others; and that on some level he did not yet understand, everything was his decision and responsibility.

My answer to her could not have been an intellectual defense or proof, because I didn't have one, although I believe that God is the only sane idea in the universe. I wasn't even sure that if there were "proof" it could be stated verbally. Another's doubt is not a condition, but a wish, and therefore cannot be reasoned away until the wish changes. So her questions were important because there was indeed something behind my continuing to act as if all these things were true.

In my attempt to answer her, this is what I recognized, and although it wasn't much, it was all the answer I had, and it was honest: I no longer cared whether what I had seen was true. Life as I had looked at it before was not worth living. It was therefore my decision to live as if this new perception was true. And if the question of whether God exists cannot be answered in the terms in which we ask it, yet the improvement in the quality of our life cannot be denied whenever we assume that God does exist, why then delay making that assumption? Why choose to be right instead of happy when there is no way to be right? I choose to make the assumption and not reconsider. A new way of seeing had been given me for a reason, and I would simply trust that.

For this was not the first time in my life I had looked God in the face. But each time before I had walked away and said, "He is an illusion." Maybe He is, but I no longer care about that. There isn't time for uncertainty. For me He exists. That is the only thing I know. And that is the reason I live.

THOUGHTS

When you find yourself in a battle with life, lose. There are no triumphs over truth.

"Rely on yourself" and "Do not rely on yourself" alone are not conflicting ideas. One must rely on what he is, but what he is is not alone.

I am not resting in Love's gentle arms while I am questioning how they got there or demanding to know why they would want to support me.

To abide in now is to abide in Love.

Love is trust in that part of me which is not alone.

There is no one undeserving of trust. Trust means I place my mind in your care.

I find my way because you find yours.

Faith is not reliance on something I would expect to be there judging by my past experience, but rather on something I sense is there because I am not judging. It is the means whereby I contact what is living now, and so it allows for an intrusion into common experience. Without it I attempt only to repeat some version of the past. Faith carries with it a mental condition of certainty and ease, provided I do not evaluate its results. Faith has no results. It moves instantly and leaves no trail. Results are noticed only when I have turned from faith back to personal history. Then I must evaluate because I have chosen the past as my authority for what will protect me.

I believe that a part of our mind foresees the entire course of a relationship before we begin it, and we choose to enter that series of events as the gentlest possible way to learn the lessons we are now ready to learn. Everything that happens between two people is by mutual design. Although this is usually not seen at the moment, it is often recognized later.

Now that I see the direction in which I walk, I find myself moving ever more often into the role of servant. And, embraced in this, which is my thanks, my world appears to be moving closer. The feeling grows, with each new person I meet: this is a long absent friend now returning. Everywhere I am noticing people drawing near to each other. An arm extends just at the instant someone thinks he has been forgotten and all that is left to him is to wander off. Now that I see there is a road, I recognize a single direction in all that moves.

There is an inherent delight and a deeply felt satisfaction in every human activity that is seen as innocent. A harmless vision is the almighty power that changes each act into light touching and a happy exchange of gifts. We feel closely held in the ripple of warmth that circles from all the human encounters around us. Every living thing is priceless and immeasurable. How obvious it is that we all do the best we can, and how blameless is each dear face.

If I look to see if I am being loved, for that instant it is impossible for me to love. Getting love is not an alternative and the attempt only prevents giving it. Love is not a matter of balance and compromise. It is totally one-sided and complete. It has no interest in effects because it already knows the nature of what it sees. Anticipation is always a judgment.

A comparison is never justified. What is unjust has meaning only when compared.

All of our differences are superficial and
meaningless; we are exactly alike.

I cannot perceive a state of spiritual
advancement beyond my own. A dark mind
cannot "see" light. What I see with shares the
characteristics of what I see. If I recognize
purity, I am pure. One true place of safety,
thought of, assures that I am safe.

I dismiss what I believe someone has done to me when I see that it is not worth thinking about.

To see the image as innocent and let it pass from the mind is to let it pass for good. To see it pass with special meaning is to tie a line to it and ensure its return. To think that an image has meaning, that it means anything, is to judge it. Say to all things: "You are wholly innocent. I understand nothing about you except your purpose to help me."

There are no neutral judgments. It does not happen that we see another group of people as different from us and yet withhold assigning a value to those differences. Prejudice has no degree. Nor is thinking that others are superior kinder to them than thinking they are inferior. Only the object of the unfairness has changed.

If I choose to think that one of my judgments is reasonable, I affirm the validity of the entire process of judging. In that instant I become a keyboard upon which all people and events play out the notes of my personal history. Everything before me becomes good or bad, interesting, boring, irritating, soothing, humorous, stupid. Every word spoken, every circumstance, all bodily and facial characteristics, every change in weather, each color or pattern, every political event, all foods, any noise or sight of any kind, calls up some previously formed judgment. I am struck by everything. Nothing can be seen as it is. Because I chose to do so, I have become a passive instrument on which anything can play my preprogrammed tune, even though there is no one else who can hear it.

My criticism of another does not contain more love than the offense I think he has committed.

All decisions are mutual.

Trying to please is another form of trying to change. Love accepts.

The content of my feeling of guilt is the same as the content of the offense I think I have committed.

A sense of personal guilt is not belief in personal responsibility but a rejection of it. Guilt is the conviction that I have become a victim of myself and must therefore remain immobile.

The attraction of guilt is that I can assign my volition to what has happened. Guilt means I have chosen to discount a broader meaning and a single cause. The ego side of me would rather be unhappy than give up its illusion that it is the determiner of the course of my life. Through opposition it maintains its sense of being something set apart.

The ego is always inventing signs of defeat just so it can tell itself it was in a fight.

There are times when the concept of "trying is lying" is not useful to me. Trying can be an easily understandable way of beginning. "You can but try" means, "Do what you can do" or "Begin where you are," or simply, "Begin." The thought that all I need to do is begin focuses my mind on this moment, which is the instant that every choice I will ever make will have to take place. Saying to myself, "All I can do is try," allows me to let go of my anxiety over how much needs to be accomplished. I will accomplish what I will accomplish, and anxiety over quantitative goals is not accomplishment.

Fear is the mood that accompanies the belief that I am capable of acting entirely on my own. Now I must defend myself and plan for my own safety and pleasure. I must "pay" for everything I get. And all my relationships shift constantly, for there is no one, no matter what his tie to me, who will not under any number of circumstances side against me. Fear is the only possible result of believing there is nothing in the universe that has unshakable confidence in me and in whose presence I am always welcomed. Fear is the condition of my mind that accompanies a deep disbelief in love.

If I seek an advantage, if I wish harm for another, if I base my happiness on someone else's inferior position, if I measure myself, my wife, my sons, in any way against another family, if I confide, if I cherish, if I criticize, if I praise, one result is inevitable: fear. I will now be thinking of myself as not one thing more than this death-bound fleck of bone and flesh with its little life and name and its meaningless little history. I will believe I am alone and vulnerable in every possible way. And I will think that any object in the world has the potential to snatch from me this pitifully small time and pride to which I still cling.

Situations are never "anxiety-producing," and anxiety is not a feeling but my interpretation of a feeling. What I feel cannot be experienced accurately simply by being named because it is not an exact match with something in the past, and a name implies that it is. To react to a feeling with like or dislike may indicate a lack of attention. I am thinking that an experience from the past, already judged as beneficial or harmful, is now repeating itself. This may be a good way of justifying holding on to it, but it does not allow me to look directly at what is taking place. For the moment, I want the form or appearance of the feeling more than I want its content. If I think the feeling is a problem, it means I want the problem more than the answer. The answer lies in the specific way this feeling can not be compared to the past.

John has just begun reaching for objects. His hand closes on something and he brings it back to his mouth. Yet once it is there, he usually sucks on his fist instead of the object. It is as if he thinks the object has become part of his hand, and that since it is new, his hand must also be transformed, and so whether he sucks on his knuckles or the part of the object sticking out from his palm does not seem to matter. Adults handle fear, grief, anger and other such feelings in a similar way. It begins with a judgment. A situation is interpreted as fearful and the mind closes tightly on the feeling of fear. Now the person thinks that he is fear. But when it is recognized that the mind has not become fear but only holds it, it is then seen that the mind is free to begin loosening its grip. This can be done by watching the fear calmly and noticing that what is watching is greater and nearer than what is being watched.

I am a mind and as mind I existed before fear and will continue after it has passed. I do not have to wrap my attention so tightly around some form of distress that I come to believe I have changed. Possibly all feelings of personal unworthiness stem from this confusion of two dissimilar things. Yet my freedom lies in the truth that what I am is still present and can be seen within a broader view. What is needed is the willingness to look around calmly and to let all interpretations be still.

What I feel is not in the present situation, or in an event now remembered, or in the anticipated future. My feelings are internal and continue by my permission. They are not originated or sustained by something "out there." They are in fact a type of answered prayer.

Resolve is a sometime thing and is not predetermined by my volition. Likewise, I am never depressed about the future. I am not a victim of what I chose before or may choose later. I pick my feelings and actions at the time they occur and in this happy fact lies my freedom.

Who told me? Who said I should be in the 6 A.M. meditation group? Do I know what is holy? Can I decide for the future what I should do, where I should go, with whom I should be, and still remain open to what is needed now? Am I quite sure I should answer every letter? Who told me that? Do I know the consequences of even one word I write? Who told me it is kind to laugh at every joke, be on time for every appointment, get less sleep rather than more, keep certain thoughts to myself, always do what I have agreed? How can I know what the situation calls for when it is clearly impossible for me to see the whole situation? Do I claim no distortion in my perception? Why then torture myself about fulfilling every unexamined claim of "conscience." Why not consider the alternative? That there may be Something within me that does know, and I can hear that Something more clearly in comfort than in guilt.

Is it really possible I will not make those contacts and have those experiences necessary to my happiness? Is there anything I can safely leave out of my attempted control?

How often is my mind engaged in manufacturing some new and ever-changing version of things to come? Certainly close to half my thoughts are so directed, while an equal number are focused on reliving and revising fragments of the past. Each reference point serves only to give meaning to the other, and my mind shuttles back and forth, raking through the past to determine what to like or dislike about my imagined future. I can find no one who will agree with my current idea of just what the right turn of events would be, but that does not cause me to question my certainty of its rightness. It is also clear that past events, similar in form to the ones I now wish for, have often failed to please me, and the ones I fear not harmed me. Yet this too does not lessen my conviction that I know what would be in my best interests. Dismissed also is the fact of my past inaccuracy in predicting what will happen, an inaccuracy so complete that on closer examination it holds no exceptions. If even this much were recognized, fantasies about the future would be of no interest to me.

The future does not seem to exist in any meaningful way. A minute from now, two days from now, it will still be now. What does now include that changing circumstances will never affect? Or possibly now is a reality entirely separate from circumstances. Circumstances must always be compared with the past, or their "implications" projected into the future, before they appear to mean anything or are of any interest to the mind. So it would seem that my mind cannot be anxiously concerned or infatuated with circumstances and still be wholly at rest within this instant.

Fantasies about the future are deceptive because they assume that time will pause. Anticipation has no meaning until my mind picks a point at which to stop the imagined series of events. The point it picks gives the "future" its meaning. It is this arbitrary freezing of the film that defines "what will happen." It never includes the question, "What will happen next?" because that would interfere with what my ego wishes the fantasy to mean. Nothing can have meaning that changes immediately, and the future never pauses for an instant.

. Time cannot bring me anything. It can only serve me now. To wait for is an inadequate use of time. It focuses my mind on something it does not have and so invites various states of rage or frustration. Waiting is a good use of time when it entails looking calmly at what is at hand and letting it pass by without condemnation or longing. This instant holds no limits on time because this instant will never end. Setting the goal of living in this instant makes of time a valuable and welcomed servant. Time itself cannot be served because it is only a means. It serves me by acting as my way of entry into life or frustration, and how I use it will determine which.

I see everyone in a different time. And I can choose another time from the one I see. Because each of us has completed the journey, it is our choice where on the road we see each other. I see no one how he is, and I see no two within the same instant. How he is, is not included in sight.

Seeing is becoming. Being is.

Therefore, see the innocence in every effort, in every act and striving by anyone your gaze falls on, and gather into your mind even the smallest evidences of gentleness. Then you will appear to become what you see and thereby remember what you already are.

There is only one dreamer dreaming the same dream over and over, each time taking a different part. When he has taken all the parts, the dream will be over.

Of course I am alone in the dream: it is a dream of separation.

Everyone I see in the dream is someone I have been. Can I forgive my past? If not, the dream continues.

Time is not sequential and continuous. Its appearance of continuity must be imposed in retrospect. Time may seem to continue where it left off, but its immediate "past" is remembered or read into the moment. The experience of time excludes peace. It is a selective memory that forgets the intervening instant of peace in order to sustain the appearance of constancy. Time includes nothing uniform except the deception that there is something more to this moment than this moment. There have been no continuously happy "times" or painful ones, because time's sense of meaning is based on comparison, and each moment of comparison causes a break, or shift into its opposite, in the "prevailing" mood.

We do not exclaim to each other what a beautiful day it is if the last fifty-six days have been cloudless. A single beautiful day is a comparison, and to pray for one beautiful day is to ask for two things. Anything longed for in this world has two sides, and to ask for one is to demand the other as well. That is why praying for worldly experiences must always yield distressing results.

We can't make the world work. There is no way to use it. We believe that if we could only change this one thing within the situation, it would serve us well. But that assumes all things will remain equal. We are now asking that they not remain equal. The situation cannot stay the same while one thing within it changes, because its very meaning depends on the contrast of dissimilar things. So after we succeed in changing "this one thing," there will arise something new in the situation that needs fixing, and on and on without rest.

In a dream, the mind splits itself into figures and grants special considerations to some and withholds them from others. Yet the dreamer himself cannot feel elation over the parts of him that have gained and still fail to be aware of loss and anger at what he has deprived himself within other parts. He attempts to solve this conflict by identifying only with the figures he has allowed to triumph, yet he can only "see" advantage by constant comparison with disadvantage. Each instant he looks at the figures of misfortune, he feels what he has done to himself, and yet he cannot stop looking without losing all the meaning he has assigned to the "good" fortune he has placed elsewhere.

I have made my experience by myself, and there is no exit from it. I am its source. I can deceive myself and believe that the misery is not mine, but I cannot stop feeling miserable. Only a wish that embraces the whole of me will allow an answer to come to this endless shuffling of loss. It doesn't matter if momentarily I feel guilty for having sought an advantage and now have wished misfortune on myself in payment. That maneuver will pay for nothing because the basic wish has not changed. When differences are no longer interesting to me, and I want instead an experience of cooperation without compromise, then I will see the real splendor of undivided caring. Now there is no wish, and therefore no will, for any other way of looking at all those who people my experience.

We all still need a little error mixed with our truth. We are not yet ready to take it straight. Since this is so apparent, why quarrel with which error another chooses to mix in?

How do I forgive? I believe it can be this simple: I just forget it.

Forgiveness and the willingness to be happy are the same.

The substance of a thought is the peace it brings.

What does "car" mean? A car in a showroom, a car heading straight toward me, a car needing constant repair, all have such isolated meanings that the name "car" cannot be said to stand for any one thing. That too is true of Scott or John or Gayle. God is in them only when God is in my mind. Only love can see steadily, consistently. Love makes one thing of all that it sees.

At any given time there are still a number of ways I have not forgiven myself, but always one I am now ready to forgive. Simultaneously with my readiness there appears in my life a person who does something I don't like, and what he does symbolizes this particular "fault." It is necessary that I first look at this person judgmentally, no matter how brief this misperception may be, otherwise I would not recognize what I am refusing to forgive about myself. He has come only to provide me with the means whereby I can see my own innocence. Another's "fault" is certainly his most valuable gift to me. It is a mirror which allows me to choose another reflection.

Having glimpsed the power contained in forgiveness, I now find myself engaging in a curious form of its denial. I am behaving as if it were much easier to forgive others their faults than their being unforgiving. I see I have made another "sin" to replace all the others. In effect, I am saying that being unforgiving is the one offense that should be held in my mind and watched over until I know that the guilty party has been amply punished. Forgiveness means "to let go." Of what? Of everything.

This will end when I see that its purpose is not punishment.

Problems are always seen leaving.

The unifying characteristic of all problems is that they end.

Free will means that whenever I wish it, I am given a way out. The door does not open to let me in. I am already in. It opens behind me. Each event, every situation of every day, allows me a newly opened door through which I can back out. It is there only because I have requested it. When escape into shadows no longer interests me, I will see an embracing circle of light where before I saw only my escape. The price of admission has been fully paid, and where I stand is already glowing. To remain requires only that I not reject hospitality by insisting that I do not belong here unless I can pay my own way in. The lightness of this moment cannot be bought with sacrifice.

To think of myself as a victim is only to hold to a wish that this situation continue. I must still feel there is something in it worth keeping and that to change even my feelings of helplessness would be to risk losing it. What is this thing I fear peace would take from me?

Events are only the external form of what happens. Form carries with it no particular content. Because I once enjoyed myself during a Super Bowl, I have concluded that watching Super Bowls causes enjoyment. Or I went to several cocktail parties and did not enjoy myself and have concluded that cocktail parties cause boredom. Anticipation is always the exercise of such illogical connections. Otherwise I would feel no urge to picture the form of future events, realizing that content, not form, is the determiner of happiness, and content is always within me.

All decisions are spur-of-the-moment. The lengthy ritual I go through of "making up my mind" has little to do with my "final" decision. It serves another purpose entirely.

Do I stand at the point of decision about what is to come, or at the point of interpretation? Possibly the only choice to be made is whether to receive my life as a gift, or to judge it and fight it every step of the way. What will "make" my life? Will it be the events to come or what I will experience within them? Is there one—even one— consistently sad or happy event?

If no mistakes have been planned into the course of my life, if all events are assured fair, and nothing can happen to violate my will, what, then, is the sense in asking for guidance in all decisions? As long as I feel a need to decide, there will be an equal need to ask. How else can anxiety and guilt be dismissed? Any need is a belief in fear over love, and the need to decide comes from my assumption that I can affect my life and others' entirely by myself. There is no real need to make a decision. I will do what I will do even though my actions may be preceded by a moment of arrogance. Still, a gentle hand will see me through it all, until I recognize that I need do nothing because nothing has been left undone.

Nothing external causes anything in the world.

All mistakes are mistakes in interpretation.

I have not been cast onto this spinning ball only to be a victim of whatever opinions I happen to bump into. Something still speaks within me. There are moments when this cannot be denied. Many versions of the truth can be heard, but there is only one truth. Whatever is going on is going on, and not something else. And I am part of that. No one is more real than I am. But if I want to pretend I am not true, I can find an endless number who will be willing to lead me in that dance, stepping on me sharply anytime my feet forget to follow my partner's personal sense of direction. Yet the mistake will be shared between us because I am agreeing to dance unequally with him.

Never do I have to find "the way." If I recognize what interests me, and follow that, it is my way. My desires will lead me unfailingly. My destiny will always remain where it can be seen quite plainly, within what I want. The alternative is to accept what I am told even though I believe it conflicts with my deepest yearnings.

At any given instant, I am turning either to the voice from within or to one of thousands coming from the world. If I hear it outside of me, it will always involve other people's arguments, interpretations and personalized reasoning. But where did they get it? If they found it within them, they will trust what also speaks in me. If it came from what they thought was separate from the leadings of their own heart, then they will not trust themselves, but only the arguments they have heard. And is there any limit to the number of arguments they have heard? What they need from me is neither my agreement nor my attack. They already feel guilty for attempting to force on me an opinion that is not fully theirs. Are speeches or thoughts from me that would make them feel more guilt what they require? They need one thing, and it will be the reason I find myself in their presence: they need my trust. Only if I see that they too have not been cast at random on the earth will I notice a certain honesty beginning to surface in all they say. Their arguments are not so strident now but more like gentle probings into my own self-trust. Take them into arms of confidence, and the selfsame arms will encircle me.

We are all saying the same thing in different words.

Any idea or technique that allows someone to let go of misery deserves my support.

Like most arguments, the one over whether God is remains an argument because each side refuses to see the other's point of view. To see it we must stand at that point and look. It doesn't matter that we think we wouldn't like the view or would find it "unreasonable." Reality is what reality is, and whatever it may be, it is so vast that no one sees it all. There would be no more intellectual standoffs if just this much were realized: we are all looking at the same thing and each one of us is seeing something. But since we are standing in different positions, our points of view differ. Fortunately, we can move. And we must if we are to see more.

In one sense, life is a process that allows us to see things in a different light. Each time our position changes we can interpret the move as a loss or gain but it is always another view of what is going on. Our personal experience appears to be divided into two parts: me and not-me. The atheist asks, "Why put my trust in something separate from myself?" The teacher of God asks, "Why put my trust in myself alone?" The agnostic is not neutral on this question, he is neutral on the word "God." The question, "What can be trusted?" cannot be avoided. Every thought and act shows where we believe our safety lies. And does anyone have that answer in its entirety? Then why not listen to what another has found to be his source of strength and freedom? Does it make any difference where he thinks it is located or by what name he chooses to call it? Is there anyone who would profess to see clearly everything included in either "God" or in his "self?"

I cannot force a change in my state of mind because force is itself mental. The means whereby I change my mind are the same as the state to which I change it.

To attempt to use my mind to change my behavior is like standing before my shadow and commanding it to move. Only my mind can change, and this is always enough.

Concern with how I behave is procrastination. Concern with how others behave is a desire for them to remain the same.

What I say and do is not separate from what I think, and that is why concern with my behavior is a decision to be powerless. To regain the power I must first recognize that my lifelong practice of fighting how I act has made me helpless. Behavior is never more than a thought. So for me to begin a war with my actions I must first convince myself that I can "act without thinking." If I could succeed in so deceiving myself, I would indeed be powerless. But if I really believed it, would I then turn around and tell my mind to send out thoughts of instruction to my body, and to be watchful for any lapses in discipline, and to remind and remind myself how to behave? If it is thought that will rein in behavior, what sets it loose? If I can decide to "be a better person," what decision preceded the behavior I now judge as having been bad? Or am I claiming a time lapse between what I think and what I do? Because thought results in behavior immediately, the only control that is ever needed is thought control, and that entails only my present willingness and not physical tension, critiques of past actions or resolutions about the kind of person I want to be. One gentle thought re-creates me in its image, nor do its effects stop there.

The mind is a movie of the will.

Concepts do not exist independently of their use. They are expressions of purpose. They direct thought because that is the use for which they were made. They do not give rest. Only peace gives rest. Concepts cannot of themselves be relied on. They will not sustain the weight of reality because they are only temporary means. They are not true but only point in the direction of truth. Properly used, each becomes a rung on an imaginary ladder that rises out of all illusions. They succeed in their task because the purpose that inspired them is real. Their function is fulfilled only when they are left behind. A concept that has not been raised to doubt has not yet served its use.

What is anything for? What is a new chair for? If someone is uneasy in my house, will this chair say, "Please be comfortable. You have not outworn your welcome." Or will it tell him of my money and my taste and symbolize only our differences?

Every thought, and therefore every word and act, is a choice. I am wanting to think of myself either as love or as a speck. As love, which joins with everything without exception, my will has no limit to its power. If I truly want peace, every mind on earth is subject to my will, for love sees no one to whom it cannot offer comfort. Each instant I wish for some form of personal enhancement, I am powerless, and nothing, not even this body, is under my control. With each thought, I am choosing to want to recognize that I am whole. Or, choosing to want some small advantage for this body before it has spent its time.

Thoughts are not random. A thought doesn't materialize out of nothing. A thought is not reason for self-reproach; it has every reason for being here. I can trust its appropriateness even if at the moment I do not understand its purpose. If I already understood its purpose it would not be here. It is here for a purpose. I am what is going on and that is why I can trust it. To dislike anything is merely to turn against my own functioning and so divide myself into warring parts. How can I be against myself and thereby expect to bring about positive change? I begin with what I am, and as a whole I take one step forward.

My state of mind leads me on a string of encounters with people in the same mental state. This is also true of Gayle's and my communication with other couples. If we are conflicted, each couple we encounter appears to have a relationship that needs fixing in some way. And when we are at peace, our world of relationships rests with us. My mind can never be a recipient only. It is at all times a participant and contributor. It is half a truth, and therefore an inaccurate interpretation, that "the vibes here are bad" or that "there is a lot of negative energy in this place." I do not find myself somewhere by accident. I have come together with certain others to exchange a thought that can be clearly recognized by all. How would I learn what it is I want if it were not for the inescapable fact that everyone around me is holding up a picture of my mental state?

Do not ask that the mirrors be taken down.
Ask only if you like what you have made of
your mind.

When our stream of thoughts is first looked at honestly, it seems embarrassingly bizarre. Who would want his fantasies and dreams projected onto a screen for everyone to see? Who would choose to carry a loudspeaker that would broadcast his every passing thought? And yet, since everyone around us also hides his mental life, we conclude that no one else but us must have such a flow of unkind, silly, weird and murderous thoughts.

As the honest observation of the contents of our mind deepens, we notice a second voice, very quiet and gentle in its message. It seems to act as a kind of reminder that brings us back to ourselves. When this is first noticed, the bizarre part of our mind distorts its message into one of self-reproach. And if one is not alert, he can easily miss the interval of peace that comes between an attack thought and the thought of self-reproach that follows. The third stage that honesty brings is the undoing of the appearance that our bizarre thoughts are random. Now we begin to sense something resembling a dialogue between cruelty and love, between craziness and harmlessness. First will come an unkind thought, then a thought that offers us peace as an alternative, then a thought of guilt for "our" unkind thought, then again an offering of peace in place of personal guilt. And so the thoughts continue like steps leading to a lovely home sitting quietly on a hill, until finally the bizarreness itself seems to take on a certain order that follows one by one the release of our fears.

Surely no one can escape noticing that the clarity of his perception is always increasing. Yet this also implies that no one sees with total accuracy as yet. As I sit here going over my diary, I am surprised at how immature were my descriptions of "the truth" even a year ago. Since this has always happened, why am I not surprised instead at my present certainty? If what I am looking at now I will soon see with much greater clarity, how can I pretend to be able to accurately describe it? How can I honestly say, "I know"? The only thing I can state with certainty about my present view of life is that it is not fully accurate and that I do not know where the inaccuracies lie. I could be wrong about anything and am probably wrong to some degree about everything. This would have to include any book I accept as my authority. Even if the book does contain the truth, can I honestly claim to understand with complete accuracy even one thing it is saying? Why then cite it as full justification for my statements? Is Truth so impotent that it would need my immature view of it as its defense?

Is there anyone who believes he was more realistic when he was younger? Has there ever been a time when I would have traded my present clarity of perception for what it was at an earlier age? Something has been happening in me that is so valuable that I would not want to see reality with the quality of vision I had at any other time in my life, even in return for every seeming advantage that being younger would bring. Since this is true, I must recognize that my self-deception was greater then than now, and that no other lack can exceed a lack of vision, for I would not return to it no matter what increase in coordination, short-term memory, muscle tone, verbal acuity, opportunities in "love" or business, or whatever other superficial gains it would appear to bring. I have been brought to a new place the value of which even I cannot escape recognizing. The remaining question is this: What brought me this far? Certainly I did not know enough to do it by myself. In fact, I would have already destroyed myself in a hundred different ways.

Something has protected me from my ignorance and has been slowly guiding me out of blindness. Can I then judge anything that has happened, or ever will happen, as capable of leading me or anyone else in the wrong direction, when I never knew enough to take even one step forward by myself?

Thoughts are strung together according to their light. Alter the light and the stream of your associations will change completely. Wish for an advantage, seek a difference, hide one desire, make a single comparison, and your thoughts will grind in darkness. Forget to judge, see past a conflict in interests, value another without limit, wait one instant in stillness, and each of your thoughts will add to an endless string of lights to delight you and comfort you and illumine your way.

Another person's voice and words can be thought of as my own speech recorded at an earlier, now forgotten time. Can I forgive what I once said? If I can't, I have not outgrown it, and that is why it is being played again. And if the words appear far beyond my present state, something impossibly out of reach, I am being offered what I have already become at a later time. Only accept this as me, and I will stride over the intervening years.

There are devices that can alter the sound of a voice. It can be made richer, tinnier or even to sound like someone else's voice entirely. There are also many ways to retard or speed up its time of delivery relative to other voices. And there is no limit to the points in space from which the same voice can appear to come. All of this can also be done with images, feelings and thoughts. And all of it can be done by the mind, as is clearly seen in dreams and other altered states of consciousness. It would take only one mind and one distortion to produce everything we experience. I now believe that this is in fact what is happening. In terms of real perception, there is only one thing going on. It has already taken place and is over. But through distortion and delay it now appears that life has countless warring parts and that I am responsible for only one of them. The I that we are is one I. Life is a lesson in taking responsibility.

How much are all of us alike? It is as if we were a "multiple personality," like Eve or Sybil, and God, our higher Self, is the psychiatrist. One day I come into God's office and tell Him that I finally had the courage to even things up with my roommate. I not only cleaned up nothing of his but for once added a little filth of my own to the room. Also, I wrote him a note telling him just what I think of him and how he will have to change if he is to continue rooming with me. Again, God tells me what He has said so often before: "Don't you see that when your roommate walks into that room, it will be you walking in? The same mind that is in you is in him. And only you will hurt when the note is read, and only you will be unable to meet the demand to change because of your belief that what is asking you to change is outside of yourself. You can only love him as you love yourself, because your self is what he is."

To look this earth over and not ask for any worldly circumstance or bodily condition different from another's is to make your deep contentment available to everyone you meet.

Who could find heaven a place of rest knowing that even one other person remained in agony? There is no comparative peace.

The ego side of me never applies ideas such as honesty, patience and responsibility completely. When nothing has been excluded from the area of its application, honesty will no longer contain an urge to hurt, patience will not be mere resignation and responsibility will apply equally to the observer.

In the Sermon on the Mount all qualifications are removed from the old virtues. A virtue is virtuous only if it has no exceptions. Who could presume to block the way of love and forgiveness while first he weighs their applications?

Kindness is not a sacrifice. My attitude toward other people can be given no more caring and generous focus than for me to ask myself deeply and without fear, "What do I really want now?"

At lunch today Owen and I talked about power, enjoyment, success and wisdom. At least this much sifted out from our discussion: The measure of power is honesty. My control is held in my willingness to look honestly and directly at whatever is before me and to think, speak and do a single thing. The measure of success is preparation. Within any event my success will be determined by the goal I set in advance. Failure can be assessed only while looking back. The measure of enjoyment is responsibility. My enjoyment lies in the recognition of my responsibility for all thoughts, feelings and occurrences, whether within me or in the world. Nothing happens to me by accident. The measure of communication is trust. Insofar as I hide from any feeling or experience, I separate myself from knowledge of reality and the love of others.

In order to dream, the mind must identify with a body or container of some kind; it must have a standpoint. Likewise, the mental image of a body carries with it a dream. If I think that a body is all I am, I am dreaming. If I think you are contained wholly within a body, I am forced to believe the same of me, and I am still dreaming. I begin to waken as I see beyond the boundaries of the body. That is why love and vision are the same.

It is pleasure if it requires a body to experience it. Peace does not need eyes or senses to be felt. Pleasure and pain are the same in content although they appear quite different in their many names and forms. The same sensation is called pleasurable in one circumstance and painful in another. To fight against either pain or pleasure merely affirms the "truth" of their evidence, that I am nothing more than a body and that my body is the measure of what life has given me. If a person mistakes me for someone else, I do not run away from him. Nor do I ask him to whisper his mistake instead of shout it. His mistake cannot change me into something I am not, so I do not attempt to reach a compromise with him or to destroy him. I simply go on being myself. Likewise, I watch the pleasure or the pain take form. I do not fear its message. I watch it calmly. And then I say, "There is more to me than this."

"I don't like the feeling of being overweight."
Proturberances do not feel bad. If the
proturberance of a large chest could feel
good, the proturberance of a large stomach
could not feel bad. Judgments feel bad. And
when my disapproval of other people's bodies
must now be applied to mine, I say, "This
extra weight makes me feel uncomfortable."
Is the answer to then spend six months
shifting the weight of my disapproval back
onto other people?

There is no inherent goodness in being thin. Virtue must be looked for in the goal. What am I dieting for? What is the purpose of the sacrifice? Isn't it to shape myself so that I will suffer less than others? Aren't I striving for nothing more noble than to be victorious in the comparison battle? Is it kinder to defeat than be defeated? To whom will my new body give comfort?

What is my body for? If my work on this earth is held in what I give and receive of others, then my availability determines my accomplishment, and my body is a symbol of my willingness to communicate. This does not mean I attempt to calculate its effect on others beforehand, but if I use it solely as an obtaining mechanism, it will not be in a position to fulfill its function. How available am I to the people who compose the stream of human encounters I travel down? How open am I to offer and accept? And what are the blocks I have placed in the way of our communication? Looked at this way, my body is the welcome I extend to others, and my attitude toward it will determine the kind of welcome it extends. I can use it for one of many conflicting purposes, and the results will be there for all to read: "My Kind of People Only," or "Admire but do Not Compete," or "I Am Interested in Only One Thing; if You Don't Have It, Don't Bother." Have I honed and adorned my body to create a need and a longing in others, or does it offer simple comfort?

How do I know what I should look like or how I should act to be accessible to those I will meet? Is the next person more likely to approach a fat man or thin, a well-groomed man or tattered, a well-spoken man or halting, quiet or energetic? Of course there is no way to know beforehand. I can only consult my wish to be open and let it choose how I dress my body now, and, later, what words to speak or withhold at the time that decision is called for. My present intent is all I need to focus on.

Any part of a body, if looked at separately, appears to need correction. To separate out anything from its context is to judge it.

Often during sex, the other person's body is used as a starting point for our fantasy. Even when our eyes look directly at it, it is seen mostly as a general symbol of other bodies. However, the reality of this particular body, with all that makes it different from our fantasy, is an intrusion that cannot be entirely overlooked even from the start. When these breaks in the sexual illusion occur, they "cause" a mild critical thought such as, "That isn't very romantic," sometimes said as a joke. As sex continues and is repeated again and again, these intrusions slowly begin to displace the fantasy altogether, and the loveliness of sex with this person becomes more like a memory. Our mind makes desperate attempts to hide itself in what is still left of the illusion in order to escape the ever dawning fact that this is a body with entirely separate needs and a physical form that is different at every point from a fantasy body. Then an instant may come when the disillusionment is complete, and during that time of emptiness, however brief, love can enter and show us something within this person that is truly lovable, and enduringly lovely. We can unite within another, but not with his body, no matter how varied and ingenious our attempts. A fantasy simply cannot be entered. But love, once recognized, surrounds us both and offers an actual place of rest fully within each other, a place of rapture where our welcome will be complete and no circumstances will ever cause it to end. Once this place is known to exist, our concept of what must be practiced and our desire to attempt only the possible is turned to a wholly new direction. We would continue attempting to enter only the fantasy when actual union with another is seen to be feasible?

The person with a new "love" is unhappy for the same reason as the person who feels left and rejected. The mood of unhappiness indicates that love is thought to have a location. The belief that someone must be excluded, that some thought or plan cannot be shared with another without consequent loss, is misery. The person who feels left behind does not really wish for the freedom and happiness of the two who now "have each other." And the one who left does not want the person left behind included in his newfound happiness. Both believe that to have more, someone must have less. When anxiety substitutes for love, it may appear to be exciting one moment, saddening the next, but it will never allow one to see all the world groaning to come together.

What is not looked at during the battle for a special love is the misery that surrounds any attempt to exclude. All the seemingly random events swirling outside are believed to have no connection with the protected enclosure one appears to have succeeded in building around his exclusive relationship. But what is in the mind is in it, no matter what corner of the mind it has been shoved into. And it will stay there until the need to force new alignments in the way we are presently coming together is no longer the focus of concern.

You do not find yourself with this person by accident. You knew what you were doing when you formed the relationship, and you were not mistaken.

No one loves anyone more than anyone else. This is not an ideal; it is a fact. No one is special. But everyone is. And our individual quality is without limit.

If I feel love for one other person, in that moment I am in love with all who go before me. And if I hate anyone or anything, that time is filled with dislike for myself and any on whom my thoughts rest. All that need be done is to unite with one other thing, to wish just one other person well, and all that need be turned from is a single dark judgment.

I have long since come to question whether I can be an emotional victim of the weather, another person's remarks or any other external thing that requires my interpretation. I have "taken responsibility" for how I react. Surely the next step in honesty is this question: Am I truly ever a victim of my body? Are fear, anger, dis-ease, etc., a separate power stored in my muscles or mental tapes, or is that concept the same old form of procrastination; just another way of delaying change? If I am truly willing to forgive another; if I am willing to see that he, just like me, does the best he can; and if I no longer have any wish for him to suffer in payment—do I really believe that something assumed to be in my body's soft tissue or the memory bank of my brain can override that state of love and force me to be resentful? Even if that something were there, who is it that issues the call for it to speak? Do memories play themselves at random? Can I love another yet be coerced by my body into hating him? Who but me still wishes to seek out and endlessly review every last scrap of evidence of his guilt?

Does love have any interest in interpreting childhood scenes of misery and applying them to the present? Do I want peace with my friend or do I want to be justified?

When my thought takes on the characteristics of heaven, I am in it.

Whenever I think I see beauty but must first do something before it will be mine, it is not beauty. To see the truly beautiful is to feel its substance deep within me, and have no accompanying anxiety. Nothing can move into my line of sight and obscure it. Time cannot slowly take it from me. And no mistake of mine will destroy it. Beauty has an easy familiarity, and in its presence I feel welcomed home.

Sight is a literal extension of one's self. Vision reaches out a hand as real as its object and transforms it into its own nature. In my presence you become what I have made of myself.

Everything is to me as I make it. As I treat it so have I created it. Insofar as I experience anything, my attitude toward it is all there is to it. I have my attitude. My attitude is my gift to myself given in the form of my experience.

What my attention is focused on is what I have. And what I have is what I think I am. And what I think I am is all that I can give to another. And what I give to another is what I teach myself I am made of. For having, and giving, and being are all the same.

What I love is what I see. That is why the question, What do I really want? changes the world.

A gift given in love will be received in love.

If there is doubt in the giving, the gift is not yet mine to give.

If your friend puts down a dime to pay, do not give him a nickel. Either receive his gift gladly or give yours completely.

To give and to let go are the same.

We are in a celestial time machine that operates by means of our inner stillness. The instant we return to the quiet place within us, all external events begin to accelerate. From within the clear circle of our peace, we view a quick unraveling of time in comic speed-up of the very course of our life. Only our sudden doubt that we may be missing out on something will return us to the halting and restless pace we had before, walking through every alley, overturning every piece of litter, in search of a dear and undefined something never found by others.

If I listen only when I am alone and quiet, I have cut myself off from all but a fraction of the Voice. Stillness does not require silence and thoughts do not require words.

What do I need to do? Always, only one thing: Recognize that I know nothing so that I may hear the Voice that now speaks. Do I want to hear the voice of experience or the voice of the living present? My heartfelt answer to that question and not the effort of listening determines what I hear.

Listen with no intent of teaching yourself the lesson, only of hearing it. Life does not ask that you learn anything, only that you not assume the role of your own instructor. To think that you know is to believe that you can act as your own guide, a contradictory and meaningless concept. To select and analyze experiences and then install them as a guide for future thinking is not self-trust but the lack of it. Your self is now. And willingness to listen comes from the gentle recognition that you are never alone.

There is a place closer to you than any feeling or sound. It is a place of stillness and quiet and total brilliance. It stands before you and deep within you now. Is there one you love who, it seems, will never leave you? It is true, but if you want to know that without any fear you must see that one in this place. For here you are welcome without any shadow of a wish that you leave. Here you cannot outlive your welcome because it is a place of life, and only love has life. It has your life, your home, your place and the one you love. It holds the one you hold and this one holds you, and everyone, and every place, forever and forever.

NOTES ON BEING
TRULY HELPFUL

SEPARATING

It is an illusion, a type of projection, that one of us has fallen spiritually behind the other. The apparent discrepancy between us has actually been asked for and welcomed, because it was believed by us both that some benefit would flow from such a comparison. Perhaps each thinks he will gain a sense of innocence by contrasting his behavior to that of the other. But that is not how innocence is seen. If there is a time for us to part, that time does not have to be worried about in advance, because it will be by permission of both, even if the means we choose to carry it out is one of great resistance, "injustice" and battle.

Isn't it a mistake for me to try to love you? I would be trying to see you as something that I do not now believe you to be, and yet, through effort or technique or persistence, hope to change myself and feel something other than what I am now feeling. All this approach can produce is the empty shell of love. Yes, I might do things for you that I assume you don't want to do yourself, and even though I don't want to do them either, I would make the sacrifice. And perhaps I would speak more quietly and shape my mouth more frequently into a smile. Possibly I would not use the words that appear critical, even if I am thinking critically. Yet all the time I would feel a vague guilt because I was not being consistent, but because it was a "good cause," I would persist. Never would I ask myself if you could be trusted to receive me as I am, because I do not even trust myself; otherwise I would not be attempting to change what I believe I feel. And above all, I would not ask myself if it is possible I already love you, and you love me, because to do that would be to admit that you also do not need to change. For doesn't my effort to love you "prove" that you do? Love does not require that I override myself. And guilt is not the motivator of "loving acts." Love asks only that it be allowed. Would I welcome a feeling of appreciation for what you have seen in me, for how unexpectedly you have kept reappearing, how frequently you have sought contact, and how, when all is considered, gently you have treated me? Or is there something I want you to do first? If I realized that all that is required to recognize the love I already have is for me to release myself from needing anything from you at all, would I do that little? Just a simple acknowledgment that I do not need your gratitude for my gifts, your agreement with my intentions, your remorse for your acts or your cooperation in this endeavor. Only my sincere wish that you continue following what speaks within you, that you take your own time and your own way and that you never feel the need to even notice my blessing, because a blessing can have no price. Just my recognition that you are free, because that is what love is.

DIVORCE

The person who is convinced that a body is all there is to him does not see love as one, but as divided in both kind and number by as many bodies as populate the earth. To that one, love itself will appear to pass from his life as another body leaves, and his situation may seem worse than dying. For me to be of any comfort to him, I must recognize that for him this is the circumstance in which he finds himself. Attempts to inform or correct him will serve only to break communication, for at the moment his safety and happiness appear to be tied to how another body chooses to behave or whether it is near.

However, he has not succeeded in putting his happiness into another's hands, but only thinks he has. The time will come when he will recognize that he has made himself helpless. My part is to be for him another choice. It is not to choose for him.

Now the time has come for me to place my trust in this one who grieves, for he will not grieve long. Love has not deserted him and possibly he will see it shining still within my eyes. If not mine, it will be another's, and meanwhile I will not make the same mistake by assigning his role as one of gratitude to me. It is gift enough to be friend to one who has been friend to others, and so prove to myself the fairness and closeness of love to us both.

AN EXAMPLE

A man's wife told him that she believed she was in love with his sister. She said that she and the woman were sexually intimate and although she was confused as to what her real feelings were, she thought she wanted a divorce.

At first he was conflicted between his desire to keep his marriage and what he understood were the teachings of his religion. He believed that his church's position was that what his wife was doing was unforgivable, but he did not know what he was supposed to do about that. His wife and sister did not share his view of their behavior and did not think it needed "correcting."

When he called me he expressed his deep confusion over what to do. He said that he continued to love his wife and sister deeply despite his outrage over their behavior, and that he found himself struggling to maintain the marriage, even though he was not certain it was best for either him or his children.

In the months that followed, the outward

situation changed only slightly, but the man's mental approach underwent a fundamental shift. In a recent conversation he said that he now felt that his marriage was providing a good atmosphere in which to bring up his children, and he was relatively peaceful about his wife and sister's relationship, which he assumed was now platonic, although he did not know for sure. He said he now had little interest in the attitude he would have to reassume and the time he would have to spend "looking for sin" in order to find out what was happening between them.

I asked him to tell me what were the changes in his thinking over the last several months. Here is a summary of what he said: He did not know if he and his wife would stay married, but that was no longer his principle concern. He had found a broader purpose, and he was now content to trust the events of his life.

Communication, he said, occurs when one places his thoughts into friendly hands. If he perceives the hands as unfriendly, his efforts will not serve to unite. If he is concerned with the consequences of his communication, if he either hopes it will manipulate or fears it will disrupt, then he has decided beforehand that he is unlike the one with whom he speaks.

Always talk as if to a friend. And do not

decide for another what is the proper response.

Who can say that someone is not going through what he needs to? Who can say he is certain of the outcome? Who knows that if he were this person he would not do the same and for good reason? Who can see without distortion just what guides another? And who would claim no connection, no involvement, no responsibility in what happens to someone within his own experience?

No one is neutral. Therefore no one is capable of judging. It is not in reality an option.

FIELD NOTES

We can look back even now and see how every step we took was meant to bless us. The events that made no sense at the time are beginning to add up, and we notice a soft helpfulness glowing like the coming sun from behind all the dark hills we have climbed over. Yet we think this event is somehow different. But is that true? Let us wait a moment and be still. Our interpretation does not have to be right. It is really possible that this too is only our next step home and is not the bitter ending that it seems.

Notice this: There is a curious pattern to the encounters you are now having, the chance meetings, the phone calls, and those who come to mind. Have you seen the gentle preparation you have been given for these exchanges? Have you recognized how appreciated is your newly discovered lack of fear by all these people who are "happening" to cross your path?

In order to hold someone guilty, you must also hold tightly to the injury that you are claiming he caused.

As a child, possibly you crawled along a wall with several windows, and you may have believed the openings above you were bringing you light. Now as you walk along the same wall, you know these are only sheets of glass passing before the sun. Love has not passed out of your life, even though the body through which you last remember its coming has gone. Look up for just an instant. There is another face, and still another, waiting to greet you. You may think it is only an old friend, or a new one, or some chance encounter as you go about your work. But Love itself has not moved, and it knows a way to come to you that you can fully recognize and share.

A FINAL NOTE ON SEPARATING AND DIVORCE

A time comes when it is recognized that nothing is gained by seeking a new partner because nothing is lost by remaining with the old one. There quickly follows a second realization: that you are not with this one by accident, and much more than romantic love or friendship is held in the foundation of your relationship.

Who, then, is your spiritual partner? He is the one you are with at the time you begin to suspect the limitless value of all relationships. Possibly it is true that there is no one who would not bless you, and you him, in a lifetime partnership. And certainly there is more than one such partnership for everyone. Yet the one you are with is not just anyone, and this becomes increasingly clear as you continue together. Remember always the gift of thanks you owe this one who has come to you so often. Perhaps he is your spouse, your friend or a relative. That is not why he is there. Divorce in any form has nothing to offer you. You do not need to pursue that illusion again. Nor is it possible for you to be a victim of another's desire to pursue it. Wait in love for this one who loves you deeply. Do not be deceived by the change in form your relationship may take. All forms change. A spiritual partner is chosen by you. Your will, because it is not yours alone, will not be rescinded.

INSANITY

We can't judge people's problems without judging people. I know a woman who was very ill and went unhelped for days because her friends believed all her symptoms were caused by drinking. Because she was an alcoholic it was thought that a specialized kind of assistance was needed and they were not qualified to give it. If they had classified her nausea, dizziness, etc., as food poisoning they wouldn't have waited to offer their help.

For someone to be truly helpful he cannot decide beforehand what is needed, and this is what we do when we categorize problems and disregard the particular needs of the people who have them. If a person is in pain it is certainly all right to offer help. If we will listen, he will show us how to comfort him. It is the person who must be remembered and not what we think we have learned about his classification.

AN EXAMPLE

A woman in her late sixties called me and said there were several men, who, at night, waited outside her windows and inside the wall that was common to her house and the house next door. They would remain there until she fell asleep and then quietly break into her house and molest her, without ever waking her. She said every night she tried to stay up, but even if she managed to remain awake until two or three in the morning, they would still come in. She said she had told her doctor about it and that she had called the police, who had come out many times but now would no longer come.

This was one of the first times someone had asked me for help who I thought was crazy, and I was slightly panicked. My first thought was that I had no business trying to help her. Possibly I should call the agency that handled commitments, because she might be dangerous. But something in the woman's voice reached out to my own sanity and I felt her deep confusion and pain. By the end of the conversation she had handed me a lesson in humanity that was so valuable I had tears in my eyes. So often we forget that people who ask our help and patience have come to bless us.

After she had told me her story and had repeated parts of it several times, I asked her if she thought of herself as religious. She said, "Oh, yes!" She told me she had prayed so many times to God about this and she wondered if He heard her. I assured her He did, but I said that it was not enough that she ask God for help, she must listen to His answer. He would not force her to protect herself, but He would guide her unfailingly. Every time she had a question about what to do, she must ask it to God and then listen quietly for the peaceful sense of direction she would feel within her.

As you know by now, I use the word "God." It has very deep and personal meaning for me. However, I do not use it if I sense that the person I am talking to objects to it. And it is, of course, not necessary that you use it even with a religious person if for you that would feel dishonest. What must be recognized, though, is that no one is completely insane. There is a part of our minds that remains totally healthy. And that part can be turned to with confidence by anyone.

I was reminding the woman of what she already knew. We had come together only to help each other remember. Together we transferred a lesson we knew well to a new part of our lives. I pointed to where her sanity could be found, but it was her call that showed me mine. My original mistake was identical to hers. It could not have been an accident that I received her call.

The police, I said, were just like her and me. They could not be expected to make no mistakes at all. But God will not fail you. Ask Him about the windows and doors. Let Him tell you which lights to leave on. Don't decide for yourself when to fall asleep but let God guide you. And ask Him to stand over you and protect you through the night. No loving parent would do less.

The woman started crying. She said no one knew how frightened she had been and what hell she had been going through with this. As she talked I realized how arrogant had been my original assumption that hers was not a "real" problem. How can we judge how bitter is another's need? She thanked me for reminding her of God's willingness, and she said, "Tonight I will sleep in peace."

FIELD NOTES

It is not his insanity that I seek to make his central concern, but his sanity. Nor am I here to give him his sanity, but only to show him mine. Sanity contains no attack.

My instructions and advice will not provide him with a steady source of strength, but his own mind will.

He has reason for trusting his mind as a whole and for distrusting it when he relies on it only in part, and he can easily and quickly tell the difference by how he feels. If he is divided between full utilization of his mind and partial reliance on other people's "shoulds" and "ought-to's," he will feel conflicted and scared. He will know he is practicing trust when he is comfortable and no one is his enemy.

I am not called upon to react to another's insanity. I do not pretend it didn't happen nor do I try to attack it with logic. I am not at all interested in our differences. What I look for is that which is clearly recognizable as me, and I welcome it like a brother. No matter how bizarre is another's behavior, I can safely assume that in the center of it all is a calm and bemused eye that sees directly into my true intent.

This encounter will be to me what I make of it.

CHILD ABUSE

To worry about what he might do in the future is a present danger to the child abuser, not a future one. It must be dealt with now in order for real change to occur. His need is to recognize that terror is a symptom of an activity his mind is engaged in. The future cannot produce fear. But an imagined future can. Fear results when the mind makes a picture of things to come and then forgets it is only a picture. Now terror is logical because the actual future is not here to be dealt with. The child abuser feels panicked knowing he is helpless to control his actions in a time that is not his. But his illusion of helplessness will start to vanish the instant he sees what his mind is doing. Now the real cause of the fear can be dealt with: that he still senses within him a lingering doubt of whether he should "give up" attacking his child.

A fantasy of attack can be as useful as one that is acted out, provided it is looked at with complete honesty. If one feels guilt over an imagined attack, some degree of self-deception is present because the attack has not occurred. Go back and look at it again, this time with one purpose: to see if attack, whatever its form, offers any benefits. Remember that guilt is itself a form of attack and that the purpose of the fantasy is not to create a symbol of one's own fallibility or of the child's, but to honestly question the value of still another conflict.

Having pictured what is not wanted, a new fantasy can be created in which the kinds of feelings and exchanges that are truly hoped for is seen. This is only one of countless ways that a good and lasting foundation for a relationship can be recognized within the mind. Words and pictures are not required, but willingness to forgive and to see all concerned differently is. Focus on seeing something overlooked before, just one thing new that makes you happy to notice.

AN EXAMPLE

One day a woman called me long distance. It took her probably ten minutes before she was able to talk. All I could hear were her occasional sobs on the other end of the line, but she would say nothing. I was anxious about our connection and thought this might be part of the reason she wasn't talking, but I felt a strong urge to simply wait. After a while I said, "There is nothing you can tell me that I haven't heard or done myself."

She had just beaten up her stepdaughter. She said this had not been the first time. I told her that whatever she had done to her stepdaughter was not the cause of the problem and that no matter how long she felt guilty about it, the guilt would not bring about a real change. She said she had tried everything she knew to control her anger but that eventually she would always fail. Could I give her something else she could do? I told her that controlling her anger was also not the problem and that the first thing she had to recognize was that anger was a reasonable response to what she thought her stepdaughter had done.

I find this is a common mistake that a parent who beats his child or a husband who beats his wife will make. He believes that anger is an inappropriate response to the situation. He does not realize that this belief is an attack on the strength and health of his mind, and that undermining his faith in his own mind will accomplish nothing. Anyone who had perceived the situation the way he had would have been angry. It is the way the situation is perceived that is the problem. Another perception will call for a different response. The mind acts logically. It is the interpretation that must change, and that calls for fuller use of the mind, not less.

The girl's father, she said, was always able to reason with her, but when she tried that, it never worked. I told her of two other parents I knew. One of them, when she got angry at her daughter, would become silent. She had on three occasions gone a week or more without speaking a word to her child. I asked the woman who was calling me if she could imagine the terror that girl might have felt when her mother would do this. Could anyone say for sure that this was less cruel than if she had beaten her? I also told her about a father I knew who never refused to speak to his son, and had never once hit him, but when he got angry would sit the boy down and say in effect, "You see, this is another example of what I have been telling you for years. You never complete anything you start and then you try to cover up your failure with a lie." The boy had come to think of himself as a loser and had deep doubts about his integrity. Could it be stated with certainty that his father had acted more kindly than if he had beaten the boy?

It is a fact that anger cannot be expressed in a kind way. And if anger is felt, it is always expressed in some way. Whatever form it takes is equally cruel.

I suggested to the woman that every time she got angry at her stepdaughter, whether it felt like rage or only slight irritation, that she recognize she was perceiving her stepdaughter as attacking her in some way, and that anger was indeed a reasonable response to an attack that seemed real. Pay no attention to the anger or to the form it has already taken. Instead, look again at what her daughter had done. Was there something else going on that she had missed the first time? Was there another way of looking at it that was more honest than before? Her perception would only be as accurate as it was fair. For example, if she could see that her stepdaughter was scared rather than malicious, then she would recognize her actions as a call for help, and her natural response would be love.

No one can return love for hate. Hate is not lovable. But people are. We can only love if we see accurately what it is we are loving. Grievances and goodwill cannot be held in the mind simultaneously because love is not mistaken in what it sees.

Sometime later the woman called me again. She said she was at home recovering from pneumonia, and something had happened she wanted me to hear. Since returning from the hospital, it had become her habit to wake her stepdaughter so she could catch a ride to school with their neighbors. This morning she had forgotten to set the alarm and got up half an hour late, feeling very sick and weak. She woke her stepdaughter and told her what had happened, and asked her if she would mind getting dressed in a hurry so that she could still catch the ride. That way she would not have to get dressed herself and make the long drive. Her stepdaughter began screaming, "No! No! I don't have time. You've got to take me."

At first the woman was outraged. She knew the girl was aware of how sick she had been. But suddenly she saw something else. Within the last year her stepdaughter had begun using makeup, and she would take a full hour to get dressed. This was not an attack but extreme fear: her stepdaughter was obviously terrified to go to school without her makeup being perfect.

The mother found herself saying, "Is there anything I can do to help you get ready?" The girl said, "Yes, you could put on my stockings and shoes while I sit at the dressing table." The woman told me she began crying as she put them on. It was the first time she had done this for her stepdaughter, and she had suddenly remembered when her natural daughter had been a little girl and all the times she had put on her shoes and socks.

It can be safely said that anytime we get angry, we think we have been attacked. And whenever we believe that attack is all that is going on, we have not yet seen the situation with complete honesty.

What is needed is not endless analysis of the other person's motives. Simply ask your mind to find a deeper, fairer way to look at what you think has been done to you. If you are sincere in wanting this, and if you will wait and withhold your judgments, it will come to you, for it is already there to be seen.

FIELD NOTES

The person who sympathizes with a battered child teaches that child he has indeed been damaged. To teach injury is not love. Love does not direct another's attention to harm but to what will promote healing and safety. Rather than reinforce his feelings of being a helpless victim, it would be far more helpful to offer the child one's comfort and confidence. A child, so encouraged, can be, and often is, the one who carries healing back to his parent. He cannot do this if he has been taught to see his parents as constitutionally resistant to change.

What does one say to a battered child? The child will lead you. Do not decide beforehand what is best. There is a way out. It speaks within the child as well as within you. It can be listened for. Echo, welcome, encourage every strain of this music that you hear. You can be safely careless of everything else.

Do not panic. Your attention has been brought to this for a reason, but do not decide the reason for yourself. This one is not mistaken in turning to you for help. But give him help, not fear. Do not warn him, help him. And let the form of the help come from both of you; do not impose it yourself. Remember that help does not always have to be given in the form of words.

Guilt is not a means for change. Remorse will not correct the desire to hurt again.

ILLNESS

There is a growing awareness that no one is a victim. Many now recognize that at least small accidents and minor illnesses are often decisions. Yet there are two mistaken assumptions that sometimes accompany the recognition that each of us "creates his own reality" and is responsible for his life experiences. They are that accidents and disease are guilty decisions and that we are not individually responsible if someone else chooses to be sick or injured. These assumptions are as inconsistent as they are unfair.

If my illness is a decision, then it begins in my mind. If it is a guilty decision and I am wrong for choosing to be sick, then my mind does not function properly and I am left without recourse or hope. But if illness is a type of question, then it will lead to an answer. If it is a means I choose to take the next step, then to judge it as a separate reality and call it sinister is to perceive only the place from which I began, the door I have closed behind me, but it is to miss entirely the direction in which I now walk.

Is any experience meaningless and unplanned? If someone calls for help, do I stop to comment on how loud he is and the shrillness of his pitch? Do I say to him or think, "There is no purpose in my hearing your cry; I find myself in your presence by coincidence"?

If I am not a victim of my own disease, can I be a victim of yours? If I say I do not want to be around your negative mental state, then I am assuming our minds connect, and, if they connect, you must be equally affected by my mind. Instead of trying to prove which of our minds is "higher," wouldn't it be more helpful to us both to say that because our minds touch, we share the problem together? That no one is guilty? And that we are here to help each other see that?

I have now removed the arbitrary limit I had placed on my responsibility: that your illness is no accident but your presence is. Now I am free to focus on healing myself rather than changing you, because I wish to extend a mental state of comfort and peace and not one of accusation. I take no pleasure in our apparent discrepancy. I wish you well. Your need for healing serves only to tell me of my own, and I am happy to accept healing for myself so I may offer it in gratitude to you.

AN EXAMPLE

A woman's cat became acutely sick. She took it to her vet who, on the basis of biopsies sent to a laboratory, diagnosed two forms of cancer: advanced lymphoma and feline leukemia. He said the latter was highly contagious to other cats and possibly to humans and that her cat should be put to sleep immediately.

The woman believed in the possibility of mental healing, and she called me and my wife to assist her. By this time, her cat had stopped eating, had started to smell and to lose its fur and had crawled under the woman's bed and would not come out. Within two days the cat seemed healthy and back to normal in all respects, and within two weeks, when my wife and I saw it, its coat was rich and radiant and it appeared more beautiful than it had ever been. Nothing can be claimed medically because the cat was never taken back for further diagnosis.

Briefly stated, the woman's approach included this change in her perception: she decided to not make healing the cat her goal. Instead, all of her choices would be in the present, and healing her own attitude would be sufficient. She would allow her quiet sense of inner guidance to direct her in everything, including whether or not to allow the vet to kill the cat.

She began to look calmly at her thoughts about her cat, and everyone who came to mind, in order to discover which thoughts were anxious and which were harmless and kind. She did not attempt to fight her fearful thoughts, and whenever she noticed herself doing battle with them she stopped. To fight them would be to claim them as part of her being. I may choose fear but I do not become it. She simply practiced seeing that anxious sympathy, defensiveness, guilt and anger did not offer her anything she wanted.

The recognition that there are no benefits in continuing a mental attack is all that is necessary to redirect the mind to peace. Peace is the state to which the mind instinctively returns.

As she practiced this, a moment came when she unexpectedly felt herself flooded with appreciation and love for her cat. It happened at a time when she was looking at it under the bed. She felt very happy and safe and she knew the cat would be all right no matter what happened. It didn't matter if the cat died because she knew that somehow it was being cared for. She walked away from the bed thinking, "Nothing needs to happen to that cat." Within an hour it had come out from under the bed and started eating, but that too seemed unimportant. She had seen something natural and completely fair within the cat and she knew she could trust it.

FIELD NOTES

Pain seems continuous only in retrospect. If watched carefully and calmly at the time it is occurring, it will quickly be noticed that there are numerous breaks in the pain while the mind momentarily focuses on something else. Then the pain is almost remembered back on course.

I can do more to relieve another's suffering by being directly and practically helpful in the way he will understand and appreciate most than I can by concerning myself with whatever mental errors I suspect he is entertaining. Kindness is whatever I perceive as being received as kindness. "He won't appreciate this but it is for his own good" is an approach that brings distressing results for both the giver and the receiver. It doesn't matter whether resentment "causes" arthritis, depression "causes" colds, etc. Even if that were so, what does that have to do with me? The state of my mind, not his, is my proper concern. In that respect, gentleness and a sincere willingness to release pain in the most appreciated way possible will do more to heal my vision than endless tinkering with another's faults.

Kindness is not a tone of voice or certain words and gestures. If guilt is behind my "kind" acts, whatever I do or withhold doing will be perceived by the other person as an attack. He will feel uncomfortable because he will sense that I think he is damaged. I wish him good because he is good.

ALCOHOLISM

Each of us believes there is something in this world that could increase his satisfaction or safety. There are moments when we doubt this, but mostly our minds are directed in some form of external search. The question we must ask if we are to finally stop judging each other is: Does it matter what form that search takes?

Our shopping list of externals varies, but no one is without one. And our lists are under constant revision as each item fails to fulfill its promise and must be replaced. "If only I had someone who loved me . . ." "If I could be the best at just one thing . . ." "If I didn't have to worry about money . . ." "If I only had my health . . ." "If I could win this one right . . ."

These are only a few of the prizes that life appears to withhold from some and give to others. It is in fact in their unequal distribution that their value seems to lie. If health were universal, who would seek it above all else? If colds were a constant, who would notice? No one complains because he cannot see at night or breathe underwater, although most other forms of life can. For something to have value in the world it must be comparable, and to attempt to gain it is at the same moment to wish another's loss.

In certain instances, such as health,

exclusive love relationships, rights and private pleasures, this can be very difficult to see. What exactly have we made our goal and what must happen to others in order for us to attain it? However, the pursuit of any external appears to be relatively innocent to the one who seeks it. Always he can point to other pursuits that he will argue are far more blameworthy than his.

But does the ranking of faults accomplish anything? Is it possible we make the same mistake in different ways, that the content of our error is identical, only the form varies? I am convinced I can be of no help to an alcoholic if I believe his mistake is greater than mine. Nor is it helpful for me to enter into a kind of benevolent competition with him in which I confess that I have more or greater faults than he. Let us put aside our mistakes and our differences and see in what way we are alike. No longer interested in being a leader or a follower to each other, we can be together find something of real value that does not require the exclusion of others? If there is no one thing out there worth having, is there something within, and does that something embrace us both?

AN EXAMPLE

After work a man and his friends usually went

to a bar to have a few beers. These times meant a great deal to him, especially because of the friendships involved, and he didn't want to give them up. But very often he stayed too long and would either come home drunk or end up in jail. He believed his family was suffering deeply as a consequence.

In the course of seeking help he decided that he did not want to give up drinking entirely but he never again wanted to use it to harm himself or his family. The question was, How could he accomplish this?

He was a deeply religious man, and one of the first things he saw was that he was walking into the bar by himself. He would never think of waking up, watering his garden, feeding the chickens and doing the many other things he loved to do in the mornings by himself. Instinctively he would turn to God and thank Him for the sunrise, the huge rock outcroppings around his house, the wonderful sounds of the earth waking up.

Yet when it came time to be with his friends, because it was in a bar, he had not asked God to hold his hand as he entered. And he had not asked God to show him how many beers he truly wanted so that he could remain a good friend to those in the bar and to his family. If in the morning he could look at the earth and see how everything God had made had been put there to bless him, couldn't he look at a can of beer in the same way and listen to God's instructions as to how he should use it to bless himself and others?

He had asked God for help but he had not listened for the answer at the time he needed it most. His own boy, whom he was just now beginning to teach how to use power tools, would not ask him for help and then go into the shop and try to figure out how to use a tool he was unfamiliar with. What good would his asking for help be if he didn't take his dad into the shop with him and question him about each step as it came?

This man used the word "God" as the source of his help. It is the word I use also, but if that word is not one's preference, it should not be overlooked that there is Something to which anyone can turn that will guide him, whether he calls it his intuition, his instinctive harmlessness, his internal guidance, his Teacher, his Higher Self, his innate knowing, or whether he chooses to think of it as some undefined part of his mind, or if he prefers to use no word at all. All that is needed is to turn directly to it and ask.

I do not know how this man's story turns out in the short run. Our agreement was that he would call me anytime, day or night, that he wanted my support. I have not heard from him recently and assume he is receiving what he needs. To occupy my mind with any other assumption would be to attack myself along with him by believing there is not a guiding Hand in all that happens to us both.

FIELD NOTES

If I find myself in hell, do I want to walk out of it or run? So many former alcoholics I meet appear to have used that form of adversity as a quick door out of hell. Is alcoholism the Berlitz course in spirituality? At times it appears so.

If there are only so many drinks a person will take before he realizes that getting drunk cannot give him anything he wants, then the next drink is not a defeat; it is simply the next drink. It is a re-asking of the question, Do I like the world I have made?—and who on this earth does not ask himself that question?

Thinking of alcoholism as a disease can be helpful if it serves as a way to let go of guilt.

It is not helpful if it only represents the choice to remain a victim: for if my problem is a disease then my cure can only be as quick and effective as the present state of the medical art, and can only begin when I am in a position to seek treatment.

The family is an alcoholic. I have yet to work with an alcoholic whose family did not show through its actions that it shared fully in his decision to go through this. They are doing this little dance, one person playing the role of long-suffering sympathizer, another, the role of accuser, another, the role of the drunk, another, the role of the young tragic victim of it all. No one is to blame, for there is so clearly no blame in it. It is not shared guilt but rather a very touching joint effort. They have all agreed to learn this lesson together and no greater heroics can be found anywhere.

SUICIDE

The person in a suicidal depression is convinced of the effectiveness of attack. The last thing he needs is for me to deepen his conviction. He is insane only because he thinks that love does not exist for him. Therefore it is no accident I am here. Love is not an argument. It is a gentle presence content to be where it is.

My function is to be sane and to be a friend to the strong core of sanity in him. It is not to convince him that the core does not exist. A great deal more than madness is at work here. His point of view, which was not arrived at frivolously, is entirely reasonable. I would accomplish nothing by attempting to weaken his belief in reason or to sell him on the inadequacy of his own mind. He has looked "out there" and seen nothing worth pursuing. He has sought to be honest with himself about this, and consequently he is very near to seeing something new. Which of us sees it first is not important. It is just as likely to be him.

He thinks he has been unfairly, but quite effectively, attacked by others, by his body and by life itself, and now he toys with the idea of taking into his own hands the power that he believes attack contains and, by using it against himself, put an end to the misery that otherwise seems endless. He is mistaken. Attack cannot offer him anything worth having. Nor does it offer me anything in my attempt to help him.

Guilt is the belief that through self-attack I can improve myself. I cannot. And it is equally mistaken to suppose I can help someone who is thinking of suicide by making him feel more guilty than he already feels; for example, by "explaining" to him how real and deep the hurt would be to those he would leave behind.

His mistake is that he has not questioned the effectiveness of attack. I cannot do that for him, but I can turn away from assaulting him or myself within my own mind and, instead, use this as a time for stillness, listening and trust.

My concern for him, if it lacks trust, is an expression of my disbelief in his instinct for wholeness and peace, and as such can only communicate hopelessness. It is his mind that will save him. Nor am I at war with the contents of his mind. I have come to do nothing more than walk hand in hand with his sanity, his reason and his love.

Insofar as my mind touches his, let it extend trust. In seeing his core of internal health, I will recognize my own, and side by side we will walk away from murder.

AN EXAMPLE

A young Navajo boy had saved his money so he could leave the reservation and move to Santa Fe to study art. He believed the Indian School had promised him a room and tuition, but after moving here he discovered that he would have to pay all expenses himself. When I was asked to see him, his money had run out, he had left school and he had been unable to find work as an artist. He believed his choice was to return to the reservation or kill himself, and he had just made one attempt on his life.

As I tried to talk to him, he would suddenly become violent and break windows or tear up his paintings in front of me. When this would happen, I would go outside and sit on the hood of my car and wait. Then he would come to his door crying and say he wanted to talk. This continued until finally he took me behind his house and showed me his hands and a pile of lumber he had broken with his bare fists. We went in and sat on his bed and he took off his shirt to show me where he had repeatedly slashed his chest with a knife. He was crying out for help in every way he could, but I had no idea how to help him.

Suddenly he pulled out his knife and in a strange voice began talking about how "they should never have made these things." I knew the knife was going into either him or me. And that is when something changed.

For the first time that day I saw—not as a concept but as fact—that this was our problem, that we were in this together.

By the end of the next day the boy had a job and he had repaired his house. He seemed calm, happy and determined.

I am convinced that nothing I said or did had affected him. Our differences in age and background were so extreme as to almost preclude that possibility. But I know that the turning point came at the same time I recognized that I was not there to solve his problem, and I am certain that feeling of our being joined communicated itself in some way.

This story had a "happy ending." It is a mistake, however, to believe that if someone chooses to take his life, those around him have failed. More than once I have been told by people I have worked with that they could sense I was not afraid they would kill themselves because not once did I try to talk them out of it.

That was not the reason I was calm. I never know what a person is going to do, and there have been times I was certain that someone had made the decision to go, and later found that he had not. I am sure that what these people sensed was not my foreknowledge of their decision, but my faith that they knew what was best for them, and that their decision would reflect this. I do not believe that death is a mistaken choice. I do believe it is a mistaken interpretation. I am not in a position to judge whether it is best that a person live. But he is. I am there only to help him see that he is innocent. Our mutual freedom and respect are the only things we have to give to each other, and they are enough.

FIELD NOTES

All deaths are suicides. No one dies before he chooses. No one begins a life without knowing how he will end it.

Death is not a blessing in disguise. The person who dies does not so disguise it. But anyone who judges it as selfish and hurtful disguises it within his own mind until the time he is ready to see its true intent.

The manner in which we die is not a coincidence. It is ultimately appropriate, a just-right symbol, but never does it indicate guilt or fallibility. Its meaning is known and determined by the one who dies and not by onlookers. No one can interpret the meaning of another's death.

The last blessing we will confer through this body will be given during the act of dying. It is our departing gift but not the end of giving. It is carefully considered and all its consequences are foreseen. The damage it may appear to cause will not be seen as damage for long, and the person who dies knows this.

The interpretation of death as the destruction of a child of God is an evil interpretation. Yet, as an event, appearing to die is an act of no greater meaning than any other act. It can be seen in the light of innocence or in the bitter half-light of judgement.

EARLY DEATHS

The one who sees an early death as a tragedy is honest and it would be dishonest for him to say that he thinks otherwise. Nothing more could be gained by attacking his view than he could gain by attacking another's, for who is in a position to know? This does not mean, however, that cruelty and senselessness are the only things to be seen in an early death. Early deaths look like tragedies because of certain assumptions we make:

That it would be unfair for someone very young to be given the choice to die because the older we become the more sanely we choose in our own behalf. **But is this really so?**

That this one who died was not more than a body and all he gave and received fell within what his body did from birth to death. **Haven't we already sensed more to his life than that?**

That time determines the size of a blessing another gives to us and this one's shorter life-span means that our share was less than others'. **Certainly not. How can we measure so dear a gift as he gave to us?**

That accomplishment takes time, and this one who died accomplished very little, for nothing of value can be done in an instant. **And yet, all that is done is done now.**

That our satisfaction and contentment are not determined by what we give but by how long we last. **One moment of giving exceeds a lifetime of waiting to give.**

Every hometown and every neighborhood block will change until they become unrecognizable. Anyone who reads this sentence will die within a few decades, and he will have lived to be told of the death of everyone he now knows or they will have lived to be told of his. Each species will become extinct and each blade of grass will wither. Many stars have gone out already, but there is no star still shining that will exceed the time the others had by much. So if it is time that measures our worth and enjoyment, what then is the meaning of "a full life," and in what sense is any life-span "normal"?

You who have seen another go so quickly, close your eyes for just an instant and remember some moment when this one felt near to you and yet was physically far from your sight. That feeling was not an illusion.

You will see him again. He has only left a little while. There was a special work that required only him and, although you don't remember now, you wished him well and gave him your blessing as he went. His thanks for your understanding remains a warm and gentle place in your heart, and whenever you wish, he will support you on your way, even as you did for him.

PRACTICE EXERCISES
AND PRAYERS

There are three kinds of prayer but only one works. The first is a prayer of words. Each sentence is like a cleverly designed key for an unknown lock. Since any combination of words might work, the emphasis is on form and thoroughness. This prayer is not spoken for the benefit of the one who prays but is calculated to change the Unchangeable. The second kind of prayer is a prayer of concentration. Now it is believed that the prayer itself holds some degree of power and is not merely a request for power. The force of the will and the force of the mind are called upon. One must use what he has been given, although how that is to be done is never completely clear. And so this form of prayer holds the same note of uncertainty as did the first. The outcome is not assured because the outcome is not now. The third kind of prayer is a prayer of the heart. It is unambivalent because the true content of the prayer itself is all that is wanted and all that is sought. Unlike the first, it is unconcerned with what words are used, and unlike the second, it does not contain an unquestioned judgment of what external change is needed. The prayer of the heart has no interest in being right or making circumstances or bodies look right. It does not try to unlock God's heart or to put a part of God to good use. It embraces God. It is a prayer of peacefulness and goodwill. It is a prayer of trust and lightheartedness. It is a prayer of deep thanks and gentle communication. All that could be wanted is held within the prayer. Now the heart is singing with the heart of God, and all the earth is a chorus.

Today, as He does every day, God has invited you to a slide show. It is an offer you can't refuse. Knowing you very well, He has prepared slides of everything you still judge. As He shows you each slide, He asks, "Are you ready to forgive this?" If your heart's answer is yes, He goes on to the next one. If it is no, He moves the slide up to give you another opportunity later. When you can finally say in complete lightheartedness that you forgive all the slides, He has waiting for you a special treat: Heaven.

What is outside of thought? If nothing is, then does anything, or any aspect of anything, remain unaffected by my thinking? Or is thought something that at most has limited control over a single body, and in all other respects is neutral and feeble, able only to acknowledge the presence of that which has real substance and power? Or can thought join with God? But what does "join with God" mean? Does it mean anything at all? Could it be that love is thought's natural content? Isn't it true that thought is never at home with the subjects of fear, dislike, pride or anything that singles out and makes lonely, that it will always return to one gentle perception that can put all the pieces back together? Even during a psychotic break or extreme bodily pain, the mind will simply not stay fixed on fear. Pain, no matter how constant it seems, has to be continually remembered because the mind keeps slipping away. Thought is never for an instant comfortable with a conflicted view of anyone or anything and yearns, even during the most intense and thoroughly "justified" hatred, to find some way to forgive and make all that it embraces whole again. What if there is no power separate from my own thoughts that can threaten my mind? What if it is not possible for me to be helpless without my mental consent? What if what I think does affect those around me? What if there are no "idle thoughts"? What if I cannot escape responsibility for anything? Would that really be a curse, or would it be freedom?

Today, as every day, you have agreed to sit in a special movie theater and play a game. The theater is very comfortable and is equipped with the ultimate in "sensurround": it simulates every sensory experience appropriate to the script. On the screen is playing a story of your life which you never remember seeing. Everything has been made so realistic that you could easily forget that it is just a movie, but the point of the game is to not forget. Anytime you start to decide what you, the main character, should do next, special equipment will detect this, and a pleasant voice will say, "It is only a movie, and you cannot decide what the main character will do next because the script is already written. So please sit back and enjoy it." If you will add one more fact to this exercise, it will be true to life: You wrote the script.

Trust yourself. This is your dream.

If heaven is a place where only innocence is seen, and yet this one who stands before you is guilty, then where are you?

Beneath every word spoken to you is a single question: Am I innocent?

Teach only innocence, for heaven is where you stand.

Perception seems to encircle you. It is a ball of images filled with sound and confusion. But notice how paper-thin and one-dimensional it is. Just behind it is endless light that is still and entirely joyous. This is your Self, the undefined something you seek in all your striving, the place of rest for all your onward-rushing thoughts, lovely in its contentment and harmlessness, brilliant in its health and peace, whole and free, and forever untouched by constantly changing self-images. Look around the surface of the imaginary bubble you have placed over you. See the changing figures that play across it; now this one is your friend, now he is not; the plot favors you for an instant only, then moves arbitrarily on; the characters are used like wooden pawns and then discarded, and all that they did is forgotten. But this is no more than a fantasy you have projected onto a little veil of vapor. Your vision does not have to stop cold at its surface. There is something actual immediately beyond. It can be seen. At first only dimly, but even this slight glimmering carries with it a peace so deep that it can never be forgotten. Practice letting the tiny bubble of confusion float away. It only appears to screen you from your Self.

As you know, God can dress up as anybody. Is there anybody He is not dressed up as? So now do you see how innocent what just happened was? Its purpose was not at all what you first thought.

There is a place where you are not alone, where your voice sings with every voice that has ever sung, or ever will sing. In this place you know that no encounter was wasted and that no face passed you by unnoticed in the crowd. Here you are allowed to choose again, and this time you decide not to discount or overlook anyone. You move quickly past no one merely to get to someone else who pleases you more. Now you cannot see a single one you do not welcome, and in the harmlessness of your vision, all return your gentle gaze.

Your confusion will last but a moment if you will not hold it from you and make of it an enemy poised to attack. Hug it to you gently, for confusion is a friend that wants you to hear a new song written for you in this time only.

Today, as every day, you are studying under a great spiritual teacher. He has in his service assistants whom he has trained to read thoughts and, through pantomime, voice and behavior, to act out the thoughts they read in perfect symbolism. Whenever one of these assistants stands before you, you will immediately recognize the basic content of your thinking. You can safely make this assumption: Everyone you meet today will be one of these assistants.

How close is God?
I am alive, and only God is Life.
I think, and only God is Mind.
I exist, and only God is.

It doesn't matter that you have been distracted. Return now to this single goal: peace within.

God is not what I want Him to be.
He does not follow my instructions.
He does not agree with my definition
of an enemy.
He does not take from others
to provide me more.
He does not call upon my friends
to do my bidding.
He is not a negative
mindlessly subtracting itself from life.
He is life.
He is my life,
and That Which moves within the spirit of
every rock, beast and flower.
He is the prince and the frog.
I yearn for good and goodness because He is.
And because He is, my yearning is blessed,
and blessed again.
And forevermore His blessing continues.
and continues.

I cannot separate myself from God any more than a gesture can break away from the hand that makes it.

Where I see only my life,
Live your life with me.
When I find only my thinking,
Think your thoughts in me.
Create in me a clear vision
Of your children's loveliness,
And hug them to me with your arms.
May I walk toward them
Only in your gentle steps.
And may I feel your hand
In every hand that reaches out for mine.

What is Love but the love,
That could pass between me
And one other person?
It matters not which person.
What is Love but the one voice
That sings in me
And everything that lives,
The beauty that settles on me
And all the earth,
Waiting only to be recognized?
What is Love but the memory
Of what I have always known
But have yet to recall,
The haunting vision of a past
I have yet to see clearly,
The only future toward which I move
Even when I think I am walking backward?
What is Love but a friend
Who has remained beside me
And never once removed his hand?
In simplicity he says,
"Forgive just one other person
And you will know me."
What is Love but the only possible outcome
I could ever wish for,
The gentle answer to it all?

So often you have been disappointed
when you got what you thought you wanted,
and yet you still believe it is possible
to act out your fantasies. But what if there
were Someone to turn to Who knew your
reactions and personal preferences so
completely that He could tell you what to do
and say, so that of all possible circumstances
you would find yourself in those which would
make you most happy, and yet would always
serve to lead you closer to home? Lovely
child of God, don't you realize that is what is
happening and always has been? Only your
judgments have blinded you to the path of
blessings on which you have always walked.

You came and called to me,
And I saw you as my newborn child.
You came and blessed me,
And I thought you were an enemy
Who had returned to mock me.
You have come in every possible form:
As my wife, my sons, my lovers,
As a thousand plants and animals,
As a hundred lakes and seas.
You were the light that broke
Quickly through the storm,
And I thought you were destruction.
You were a shoal placed under the water
For me to stand on,
But I thought you were a devourer.
Now I see you stand in all things before me.
Your blessing utterly surrounds me.
I am here.
I am ready to take your hand
And come home.